STRESS MANAGEMENT
TRAINING
A GROUP LEADER'S GUIDE

**Nancy Norvell, PhD
and Dale Belles, PhD**

Professional Resource Exchange, Inc.
Sarasota, Florida

Printed in the United States of America

Paperbound Edition ISBN: 0-943158-33-8
Library of Congress Catalog Number: 89-62711

The copy editor for this book was Evelyn Tucker, the
production supervisor was Debbie Fink, the graphics
coordinator was Laurie Girsch, and the cover designer
was Bill Tabler.

ACKNOWLEDGEMENTS

We wish to thank the many people who have helped us refine our stress management program. In addition to numerous individual patients and occupational groups, many fine therapists have assisted us in developing our ideas. Thanks go particularly to Holly Hills, Phil Hanger, Jill Samo, Anne Fruend, Stephanie Brody, and Eric Mings. Several authors have also inspired us with their writings, including Don Kiesler, Jim McCullough, Don Meichenbaum, and Jim Johnson. We would also like to thank our editors, Peter Keller and Larry Ritt, for their encouragement of our efforts. Finally, we dedicate this guide to two special people, Tim Boaz and Laura Mee.

N. N. and D. B.

TABLE OF CONTENTS

INTRODUCTION

Originally, we began writing this guide to accompany the *Stress Management Workbook for Law Enforcement Officers*. We wanted it to be an elaboration of the techniques outlined in the officers' manual and to provide the background and rationale for these techniques. However, our experience with a variety of occupational groups has proved the applicability of this material to diverse professions. The techniques described here have been successfully implemented repeatedly with individuals and groups of widely varying occupational backgrounds. Consequently, we encourage you to examine and utilize the material and adapt it as needed to the specific occupational group(s) and individuals with whom you are working. We have written this guide so that it may be used by a wide range of professionals, including directors of employee-assistance programs, counselors, personnel supervisors, and mental health professionals.

As a stress management facilitator, it is important that you understand what is known about stress and its treatment. Over the past 10 years, the concept of stress has become a popular explanation for a wide variety of psychological and physical complaints. Indeed, research has indicated that stress may be a causal factor in a number of medical and psychological difficulties. It is also known that stress can exacerbate existing problems. Consequently, a variety of "solutions" have been offered under the rubric of "stress management." Although several effective approaches have been developed (see Woolfolk & Lehrer, 1984, for a review), a great deal of work is still needed to *define* more precisely the concept of stress, to identify more clearly the impact it can have on people, and to continue to develop effective stress-reduction techniques. Based on what is known, we offer a program with a theoretical background and a practical approach to helping people deal more efficiently with stress. We encourage you to review this guide before initiating your stress management program and we welcome your comments.

Nancy Norvell
Tampa, FL

Dale Belles
Atlanta, GA

October, 1989

STRESS MANAGEMENT
TRAINING
A GROUP LEADER'S GUIDE

CHAPTER 1. STRESS AND ITS MANAGEMENT

Although many people feel they are well acquainted with the experience of stress, it is a difficult concept to define precisely. Pioneers in the field emphasized the physiological changes associated with "physical stress." Hans Selye (1956) developed a theory of stress, which he called the general adaptation syndrome, and demonstrated that regardless of the type of stressor to which his laboratory animals were exposed (prolonged immersion in ice water, severe burns, etc.), there was a predictable consistency in their physiological responses. Selye and others later examined the effects of stressors that were not direct physical threats. A large body of literature has focused on "life stress," or those life situations that lead to physical and emotional difficulties. Holmes and Rahe (1967) devised a scale by which individuals could calculate the amount of significant changes (both positive and negative) to which they had to adjust over a certain period of time. Several studies confirmed that higher life stress scores were associated with illness and disease.

However, this conceptualization of stress, much like Selye's early work, emphasizes a very "external" orientation. In other words, events occur over which we may not have control (e.g., death of a spouse), and this causes the experience of stress. It is a somewhat pessimistic conceptualization of stress as it implies that the people have very little control over events with which they have to cope. Other stress researchers felt that the experience of stress could not be adequately explained simply by the occurrence of an event that required adaptation. Sarason,

1

J. H. Johnson, and Siegel's approach to life stress (1978) differed from that of Holmes and Rahe in that it assessed individuals' life stress by asking them not only to identify the occurrence of life events, but also to categorize events as desirable or undesirable and then to rate the impact that the events had had on them. Thus, a "negative" change score could be calculated that provided the sum of the impact ratings of those events experienced as negative. This was a very important theoretical development in the area of life stress measurement as it emphasized the individual's cognitive appraisal of the event (how negative and how much impact) rather than only the event itself. In many ways, this is a more optimistic view because it emphasizes that while we cannot necessarily control life events, we can have an effect on how we interpret and cope with them.

How does a person learn to cope with life stress? A variety of stress management approaches have been devised to assist people in dealing more effectively with stress. It is not surprising that most approaches incorporate a cognitive component that focuses on the individual's attributional processes (i.e., what the event *means* to the individual). However, unlike Selye's laboratory animals, not everyone experiences consistent reactions following a stressor. Physiological, cognitive/emotional, and behavioral changes have all been identified as possible reactions to stress. Comprehensive stress management programs that teach a variety of coping methods seem most feasible, especially since researchers have not yet been able to identify which techniques will be most effective for which individuals.

There are many, many potential stressors, and a broad-spectrum stress management approach should teach stress management skills that are applicable to a wide variety of stressors. As attention has been drawn to stress and its potential adverse effects, one particular area of interest to emerge has been the development of programs to help employees identify and deal more effectively with stress as it relates to occupational demands. Stress management programs offered to workers can be viewed as health-promotion efforts similar to smoking cessation or weight reduction programs. Negative health-related behaviors which affect productivity, health, and early mortality are estimated to cost employers millions of dollars each year. The National Institutes of Health estimated in 1981 that the 26 million work-loss days resulting from cardiovascular disease translated into a $1.2 billion loss in earnings. As employee health-care programs have become more inclusive, many companies are finding that the health of their employees constitutes the difference between profit and loss (Girdano, 1986). Evaluation of the specific advantages of health improvement programs aimed at reducing negative health outcomes such as hypertension, obesity, and smoking indicates a general trend toward cost effectiveness for improving job performance (Fielding, 1982).

Employers have also begun to offer broader treatment programs for stress management that comprise a myriad of techniques designed to help individuals exert greater control over their physiological and psychological reactions to stressors. Murphy (1984) reviewed and appraised 13 studies of work-site stress management programs and offered tentative conclusions that they were beneficial in teaching workers how to exercise greater control over physiological and psychological systems that may contribute to stress. When critically examining the occupational stress management literature, it is important to keep in mind that subjects may or may not have demonstrated maladaptive physiological, cognitive, or behavioral responses to stressful stimuli, and prevention, not remediation, has typically been emphasized. It is widely held that, as indicated in the title of one physician's report on stress management programs, "Promoting Health Is Good Business," these stress management programs can facilitate job productivity and reduce the likelihood that employees will turn to less adaptive ways of coping (Reinertsen, 1983, p. 18). There is also evidence that work-site interventions can reduce absenteeism and facilitate employees' willingness to adopt more positive health-related behaviors.

In addition to viewing stress management as a health promotion approach that employers may endorse, the treatment of stress can be specifically focused on occupational demands. Job stress has been defined as "the sum total of factors experienced in relation to work which affect the psychosocial and biological homeostasis of the worker" (Weiman, 1977, p. 119). Job stress, in particular, has been associated with a variety of health consequences, including coronary heart disease, hypertension, diabetes, and ulcers (Cobb & Rose, 1973; H. J. Russek & L. G. Russek, 1976; Sharit & Salvendy, 1982). Specific stressors that may contribute to job stress include products of the

3

physical environment, demands of a specific occupation, group and organizational relationships, and outside influences such as family problems and economic difficulties.

The term "burnout" has been coined to describe the undesirable consequence of not coping effectively with job stress. Burnout has been characterized as a syndrome of emotional exhaustion, depersonalization, and lack of personal accomplishment that occurs in response to chronic stressors generated by the organization (Maslach & Jackson, 1981). The importance of the burnout concept is suggested by its relationship to undesirable occupational consequences such as job turnover, absenteeism, low morale, medical and disability costs, and poor performance (Maslach, 1982). The specific characteristics or demands of occupations that have been described by researchers as contributing to burnout and occupational stress include low pay, overwork, unsupportive management, lack of recognition for job performance, and conflictual or isolated work environments (Taber, 1984).

Although job stress may be the focus of your stress management program, the program we outline here, like most stress programs, is not designed to address problems best handled through organizational change or job redesign. Certain stresses associated with particular job requirements may be unavoidable (e.g., shift work, heavy work load, etc.) and thus not amenable to change.

STRESS MANAGEMENT: IN WHAT FORM AND FOR WHOM?

If stress management is viewed as a way of improving coping skills as a preventive measure, then it may appear that everyone could benefit from learning techniques to reduce stress. After all, stressful life events often cannot be avoided or controlled. The techniques we cover are not difficult ones to grasp, and it may be tempting to offer stress management programs indiscriminately for individuals or for groups. While extensive clinical education and training (e.g., a PhD degree in psychology or an MD in psychiatry) are not necessary to learn and teach stress-reduction techniques, such training is extremely useful in understanding and identifying which persons can benefit from this approach and which need psychological intervention beyond a stress management program. The techniques can be incorporated into an individualized program, but a group format is probably more cost-effective if potential members are adequately screened. In addition, being in a group may make the sharing of mutual occupational frustrations by co-workers easier. A group format also allows employees to learn from one another as they develop new problem-solving strategies to cope with stressors.

Group cohesiveness among co-workers (Mattingly, 1977) and staff meetings that allow for sharing of experiences and social support (Maslach & Pines, 1977) have resulted in decreased emotional exhaustion in employees, further supporting the use of the group modality for occupational stress management. A stress management group can be viewed as a class for individuals who are generally coping with their current stressors. In other words, they are not experiencing major psychological symptoms - that is, they are not experiencing major occupational or social disruptions - and there is no indication that individual psychotherapy is warranted. If you offer a program for a specific occupational group (e.g., nurses, law enforcement officers), there are different factors to consider related to group membership and screening. However, when offering a program to a more heterogeneous population, we suggest that you meet on an individual basis with each potential group member to assess the following issues.

1. *The individual's current stressors and reasons for participating in a stress management group.* Persons who are focusing on one major life stressor (e.g., the recent death of a family member or being fired from a job) are likely to be experiencing distress specific to that stressor and most likely need individual attention. Other indications that individual treatment is warranted include such comments as, "I feel I'm at my rope's end," "Nothing is working for me," and "Stress is affecting a lot of different areas in my life (e.g., not eating, not sleeping, being afraid to go out of the house)."

2. *Experience with psychological/psychiatric treatment.* If currently in treatment, the person should discuss the appropriateness of the group with his or her therapist. Significant psychiatric history (inpatient hospitalizations, psychotropic medications, alcoholism or drug abuse) are also indications that the stress management group is not appropriate.

5

3. *Commitment.* You need to assess whether the person can commit to attending all sessions and possesses the motivation to learn active coping skills to help deal with stress. Individuals need to understand that reducing stress means making a commitment to make changes and learn new skills, not simply griping and venting frustration concerning employers and the organization.

4. *Individual factors.* Although your group may be heterogeneous in terms of occupational status, age, marital status, and the like, there are some areas in which members should be similar. For example, you will want to gear your presentation of the material and techniques so that it is appropriate to the intellectual level of the group. Someone significantly more or less intelligent than the rest of the group may be dissatisfied or frustrated. While individuals from diverse occupations can generally interact well, you may want to consider potential problems in mixing obviously disparate occupational groups. If occupational stressors become a focus, you may find too much diversity.

In addition, you want to assess individual factors that may have an adverse effect on the group. For example, persons who are very controlling or long-winded may tend to dominate discussion and consequently bore or intimidate others. People who are extremely pessimistic or negativistic may also undermine other group members' confidence in the program. Individual counseling may be more appropriate for such people.

Finally, we recommend that the group remain rather small in size, generally between 6 and 12 people, to facilitate involvement and discussion on the part of all members. To foster trust, candor, and confidentiality, we generally advise against including supervisors and subordinates in the same program.

CHAPTER 2.
EXPLAINING THE
CONCEPT OF STRESS

In helping people to cope with this monster called stress, it is important that you have them discuss their own experiences and what they find stressful in their lives. In a group format, participants are typically reluctant at first to talk about stressors of a personal nature and will probably focus on stressors associated with their jobs until they feel more comfortable with the group. Rather than just describing specific stressors, you will want them to feel they can define stress. As mentioned in Chapter 1, however, defining the abstract concept of stress is a formidable task.

Begin by asking members to define "stress." If you are working with a group, write down all responses on a blackboard. You will find some people offering consequences or symptoms, or the response definition (e.g., feeling tired or depressed, unable to be excited about anything, bodily tension), whereas others will describe situations, or the stimulus definition (not getting a job promotion, having to go to work on their day off). In all cases, be sure to offer reinforcement for their efforts (e.g., "That's a good one" or "That's an interesting way of looking at it"). All of these responses will be useful and can be labeled later when you explain behavioral, physiological, and emotional responses in the stress-illness model.

Next, you will want to give some historical background of how we have come to understand stress. You may begin by talking about two important pioneers in stress: Hans Selye and Walter Cannon. Explain to participants that it was Selye's early work that helped scientists to realize that the physiological responses were similar despite the different sources of stress (Selye, 1956). "Stressors," as he defined them, were physical threats to the organism - things like being in a fire or nearly drowning. He exposed animals to a variety of stressors and found that whatever the source of the stress, they responded in a similar physiological way. He identified a three-phase process (alarm, resistance, and exhaustion), which he termed the "general adaptation syndrome." Consequently, he offered a definition of stress as "the nonspecific response of the body to any demand made upon it" (Selye, 1974, p. 14). This definition emphasizes that change (anything requiring adaptation) can cause stress. Later, Selye (among others) further developed this concept, and we now recognize that even positive events (job promotion, Christmas, etc.) can also be stressful because they, too, require a certain amount of "adaptation energy."

The next point you will want to make involves the fight-or-flight response, particularly emphasizing how stress in our world today differs from the kinds of stress that our ancestors experienced. Thousands of years ago, our ancestors lived in a world in which life-threatening situations were a routine part of life - for example, confronting wild animals who were looking for their next meal. A person out for a walk who unexpectedly encountered a ferocious animal would experience many changes in his or her body, including increases in heart rate, blood flow to the muscles, and adrenaline. Such physiological responses helped people to prepare to stand their ground or to flee the aggressive animal. Similarly, this "wired-in" response can be adaptive today. You might wish to give the following example to illustrate how this response helps us in today's society.

Let us say you respond to a noise in the garage, which you suspect might be made by a prowler. In the dark shadows, you suddenly see a very large shadowy figure. Sensing danger, but uncertain as to who (or what) the figure may be, you, too, would experience many changes in your body. You might hear your heart pounding as your heart rate increases, your breathing would quicken, your palms might begin to perspire, and your muscles would probably tense up. Again, this would be adaptive in that these bodily changes would be preparing you either to fight off this potential aggressor or to flee.

Unfortunately, this response is not always adaptive. Many of our modern stressors are not life-threatening; more important, they are not well suited for the fight-or-flight response. For example, it generally *is not* adaptive to flee (or fight) when a boss makes unreasonable demands. By providing this rationale for your participants, you are laying the groundwork for helping them understand the necessity for developing new coping strategies.

By this point you should have hooked them into believing that the fight-or-flight response does not always work. However, they may be unable to understand why they should not just keep dealing with stress by using other methods (e.g., keeping their mouths shut, having an extra drink at home). Here is where the stress-illness model (modified from Greenberg, 1983) can help individuals understand the many negative consequences of stress. Your presentation of the model will also introduce the cognitive element in stress - in other words, how people *perceive* the event. The model consists of a life event (stressor); perception; emotional, behavioral, and physiological responses; and then illness/disease (psychological/medical).

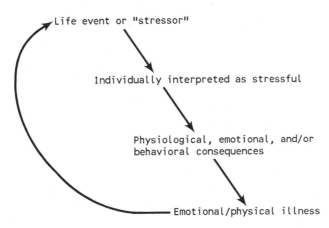

As you explain the life event (stressor), you should emphasize that what is stressful for one person may not be for another. Originally, stress researchers believed that certain events were inherently stressful *at the same level* for all individuals. At this point, you may want to talk about the social readjustment scale, as some of your participants probably have heard of Holmes and Rahe's list of events that provided a "score" (life change units) for all kinds of events (Holmes & Rahe, 1967). The list included not only major negative events (e.g., death of a loved one), but also minor hassles and positive events. As we mentioned earlier, persons who equate stress with external events may be pessimistic in believing that they are unable to have an effect on their own stress levels. For this reason, it is important to focus more on the approach taken by Sarason, J. H. Johnson, and Siegel (1978), which emphasizes that it is not the actual event that is stressful (and leads to psychological and physical problems), but how the person views or interprets the event. We do not have control over many events, but we do have control over how we view things. Objectively, no one would enjoy being denied a job promotion, but the consequences will be much different for the person who catastrophizes about the event (self-statements like "I know this is it. I'm screwed again - I might as well give up") as compared with the person who confines disappointment to the specific event ("I'm disappointed I didn't get the promotion. I need to think about what I can do to get the promotion next time").

You will then want to provide examples of the responses that follow the perception. This is another time to utilize the blackboard and encourage participants to identify different stress arousal cues (behaviors like overeating, sleeping too much, yelling at people; emotional reactions like frustration, anger, depression, irritation, aggressive feelings, hate; and physiological responses like an upset stomach or tension in the neck). Some of the symptoms are physical changes within the body (the familiar fight-or-flight responses, including increases in heart rate, blood pressure, breathing rate, and muscle tension). Also produced are changes in the body's immune functions. Other consequences are emotional or psychological (anxiety, fear, anger, and depression). Have participants consider how they feel after an argument with their spouse or after having witnessed a major accident involving the loss of life. Even feeling "numb" or "nothing" is an emotional response. Explain that we all respond to stressors on some emotional level even though we may be very good at hiding it from others. Point out that sometimes people are even unaware of or unable to label their emotions.

Last, there are behavioral consequences associated with stress. Explain that if we are operating under a lot of stress, we are more likely to engage in other maladaptive behaviors that can contribute to illness as well as actually lead us to feel even more stressed. For example, we may sleep less, eat poorly, or drink more than usual - all are behaviors that can increase susceptibility to illness and are therefore maladaptive. When we feel stressed, it becomes even more difficult to change bad habits. For example, we say to ourselves, "I know I should stop smoking, but I just don't have the will power," or "Maybe I should lose a few pounds but eating is one of my few pleasures," or "I should get back to exercising regularly, but I just don't have the time or energy." It is important to confirm for participants that we all experience these stress consequences periodically, and, in fact, a little bit of stress and physiological arousal can help us motivate ourselves to assume our responsibilities. However, when these changes continue and become chronic, they can lead to such lingering emotional changes as depression or anxiety, the weakening of various organs within our body, and ultimately *physical illness or disease* or maladaptive behavioral patterns such as alcohol abuse or poor performance on the job.

Finally, we come to the illness. Point out that research has revealed an association between prolonged stress and some illnesses, including heart disease, stroke, high blood pressure, ulcers, tension headaches, backache, asthma, arthritis, and even cancer. Here you may want to provide a detailed example of how an illness might develop as a result of stress. One such example might be hypertension (high blood pressure). Although the exact mechanism of how hypertension develops is poorly understood, one model emphasizes the fight-or-flight reaction to mental stress, which involves the sympathetic nervous system's activity and its effect on the cardiovascular system. Sympathetic activity results in an acute rise in blood pressure by constricting blood vessels, increasing skeletal muscle tone, and restricting blood circulation in the kidneys. This leads to a release of the hormones renin, angiotensin, and aldosterone from the kidneys and brain, which further elevate blood pressure via sodium and water retention, and further blood vessel constriction. Sustained increases in blood pressure serve to reset mechanisms called baroreceptors (thermostat-like sensors in the heart and arteries that regulate blood pressure). The baroreceptors would normally cause the heart rate to slow and peripheral blood vessels to dilate to counteract the high blood pressure. However, the continued elevation in blood pressure resets them at a higher level so that even higher levels in blood pressure are needed to cause the baroreceptors to respond and lower blood pressure. Persistent elevations in blood pressure may also change the resiliency of blood vessels, which, in turn, affects blood pressure levels. Thus, the continual responses to stressful events may eventually lead to hypertension.

Of course, illness (psychological or physical) may not necessarily be the end point. In fact, illness is often a stressor and can start the cycle again.

IS ALL STRESS BAD?

At this this point, you have emphasized the potential negative effects of experiencing stress on our emotional and physical well-being. However, that does not mean that all stress is bad. We experience stress every minute of our waking lives. It may be very slight or very intense, but it is a fact of life. As mentioned previously, some stress is considered necessary to energize us to perform vital activities. You will want to emphasize to participants that their goal should not be to eliminate all of their stress. Too little stress would result in boredom and monotony. Research has shown that stress is a double-edged sword. Too much stress increases the risk of illness and decreases work performance. Too little stress has been shown to be related to lack of motivation, apathy, and boredom. It appears then that there is an optimal amount of stress people need in their lives to motivate and maximize performance. The key for participants is to understand what is being experienced and how to respond to specific stressors in their lives. They will then be able to intervene to manage to keep their stress levels comfortable.

SIGNS AND SYMPTOMS OF STRESS

After providing some background and definitions related to the concept of stress, individuals should be given the opportunity to discuss their views of stress. Next you will want to personalize the program a bit more for them. The first step toward effective stress management is *awareness*. While you may vary the emphasis of different components of the program depending on the amount of time you have, the format, and the audience (individual vs. group), this portion is one that should not be shortened. Perhaps the single best intervention that can be made is helping individuals identify their own *specific* reactions: cognitive components, what behaviors they engage in, their bodily responses, and their emotions. As a way of increasing awareness, have participants fill out the Stress Response Index (pp. 15-16). Once they have completed this exercise, solicit discussion of individual responses to stress. This exercise serves to normalize the varieties of responses to stress, and will encourage the individuals in identifying stressful events that will be analyzed later.

After focusing on increasing awareness of their own symptoms, you may want to direct a portion of your presentation to recognizing stress in others. Here we try to emphasize that while there may be some similarities in the type and frequency of stress symptoms, there are also some differences among individuals. Many of the physiological, emotional, and behavioral signs are ones of which only the individuals themselves can be aware. For example, it is difficult (if not impossible) for a co-worker to recognize that a colleague's heart is pounding or that the person is having troublesome thoughts that will not go away. Some of the signs are subtle but can be observed. Point out that one of the simple keys to identifying stress is change - is the person (or the co-worker) acting "differently" than usual? But simply encouraging participants to look for any or all kinds of changes is not helpful advice for two reasons. First, it is difficult to identify "change" - we need specific signs to look for. Second, these changes can take place very gradually. For example, a co-worker may have had a very difficult time adjusting to a transfer to a new agency, or even to a different department within the same agency, but did not want anyone to know and so kept quiet and worked very diligently. Yet the person may have been spending more nights out at bars, and drinking an increasing amount of alcohol. It could take many months for a colleague to realize that this person had a drinking problem, and by that time it might be much more difficult to intervene. Have participants read through the Stress Cue Identification (p. 14) list and discuss several instances when they have seen these cues in people they knew. This list is a bit different than the Stress Response Index as it emphasizes those signs that an outside observer might be able to identify in other persons.

13

STRESS CUE IDENTIFICATION

<u>Physiological Responses</u>

- vague physical complaints
- stooped posture
- sweaty palms
- trembling
- dilated pupils
- chronic fatigue
- body motions indicating arousal (tapping foot excessively, etc.)
- weight gain or loss

<u>Emotions</u>

- apparent sadness
- apparent anger
- easy distractibility
- daydreaming
- frequent mood changes

<u>Behaviors</u>

- explosive outbursts
- impulsive actions
- complaining
- negative statements
- cynical or hostile remarks
- self-critical
- overly critical of others
- withdrawn/ difficult to communicate with
- talks about the past much more than the future
- increased use of alcohol, drugs, tobacco, or caffeine
- insubordinate to superiors
- change in job productivity
- lack of attention to details

STRESS RESPONSE INDEX

0 = This symptom rarely or never occurs.
1 = This symptom occurs occasionally.
2 = This symptom occurs quite often.
3 = This symptom occurs all the time or nearly all the time.

<u>Physiological Symptoms</u>

____ racing or pounding heart
____ rapid breathing with short, shallow breaths
____ cold sweaty palms
____ excessive perspiration
____ asthma attack
____ butterflies in stomach
____ nausea
____ constipation
____ diarrhea
____ dry mouth
____ high blood pressure
____ sudden and urgent need to urinate
____ tics or twitching muscles
____ heartburn/indigestion
____ stomach cramps or pains
____ tremors or shakiness
____ headaches
____ back pain
____ change in appetite
____ impaired sexual function
____ chronic fatigue, exhaustion
____ frequent urination
____ arthritis pain
____ weight change
____ itching
____ dry skin
____ allergy flare-up
____ colds or the flu
____ skin rash
____ other; specify _____

<u>Emotional Symptoms</u>

____ difficulty concentrating
____ feelings of being sad, blue, or down in the dumps
____ feelings of anxiety, panic, or being out of control
____ forgetfulness
____ suspiciousness
____ racing thoughts

Emotional Symptoms (Continued)

____ recurring thoughts you cannot get rid of
____ inability to enjoy the things you used to enjoy
____ feeling as if you will explode
____ restlessness
____ diminished ability to daydream or fantasize
____ mood swings
____ decreased interest in sex
____ decreased interest in previously enjoyed foods
____ being withdrawn, socially isolated
____ apathy
____ cynicism
____ other; specify _____

Behaviors

____ erratic work habits
____ increased use of sick time
____ excessive worrying
____ excessive use of alcohol or other drugs
____ excessive accidents or injuries
____ overeating
____ excessive complaints
____ crying
____ increased craving for tobacco or sweets
____ change in sleep patterns (difficulty falling asleep and/or waking up more frequently during the night)
____ angry outbursts
____ nightmares
____ lack of punctuality for work and/or other important appointments
____ gritting teeth
____ nail biting
____ finger or foot tapping
____ other; specify _____

CHAPTER 3.
PRESENTING INTERVENTION
TECHNIQUES

RELAXATION TRAINING

While a common-sense solution to stress is *relaxation*, this is no easy accomplishment. For years, physicians (particularly cardiologists) have told their patients, "You need to relax." However, this prescription to "go relax" is about as easy for most patients as to "go lower your blood pressure." The big question, of course, is *how*? Relaxation is a skill that must be learned and, like any other skill, requires practice. Before going through the procedure, spend some time on the rationale, particularly emphasizing how it can counteract the physiological fight-or-flight responses.

Numerous variations of relaxation training are described in the literature, but one particularly popular technique is progressive muscle relaxation (PMR), described by Bernstein and Borkovec (1973). PMR is a shortened version of Jacobson's (1938) procedure. You should describe PMR as a portable stress-reducing technique that involves learning to become deeply relaxed at any time it is desired to do so. Its goal is to combat stress by producing responses in the body that are incompatible with stress. That is, your body cannot be both tense (stressed) and relaxed at the same time. It is particularly useful for helping reduce the bodily symptoms of stress, such as tension in specific muscle groups. When a person feels tense, upset, or nervous, certain muscles in the body tighten. Progressive muscle relaxation training consists of learning to relax the major muscle groups of the body by sequentially tensing and relaxing them. While doing so, it is important to pay close attention to the bodily feelings associated with tension and relaxation. Instruct participants that they will learn to recognize the bodily signs of tension in their bodies and eliminate it whenever they choose to do so.

Some participants may have had previous experience with this or other relaxation techniques. Encourage them to discuss their experience and reassure them that PMR is a particularly well-researched technique with documented success.

However, many participants will not have had any experience with relaxation training and so, it is especially important to prepare them for the sensations they may feel. Warm and tingling sensations are often reported, particularly in the extremities. Some report that their limbs feel heavy whereas others claim a pleasant floating sensation. Intrusive thoughts can usually be managed by refocusing attention on the task at hand, namely, the feelings in the body.

Many individuals are skeptical when they first learn about relaxation techniques. They may view them as some strange "far-out" approach. Some also view them as hypnosis. They may fear losing control and are wary of any technique where they may not be in control. Emphasize that they are learning a method that they can use to reduce stress - relaxation training is not something that is "done" to them.

Next, go through the procedure with members. Before beginning the exercise, ask participants to loosen tight clothing and to sit comfortably in their chairs. Eyes should be closed or focused on a specific spot (e.g., a light switch). Dim the lights and make the room as quiet as possible. The following is an example of how to conduct the procedure. There are many varieties of relaxation training, and this "script" is based largely on the Bernstein and Borkovec (1973) progressive muscle relaxation technique.

"Try to find a comfortable position in the chair. As you do so, focus only on the task at hand, namely, becoming keenly aware of the feelings inside your body. Focus only on what is going on inside your body; try to put all of your other worries out of mind while we go through this procedure. As we go through this relaxation exercise the first time, I will be guiding you step by step. As you become more proficient with the procedure, you will be able to produce pleasant feelings of relaxation on your own at any time you desire. To be sure you will be comfortable, loosen any restricting articles of clothing or jewelry such as ties, watches, or belts. As you sit comfortably in your chair while focusing on the feelings inside your body, focus all of your attention now on the first muscle group, the right forearm and hand. Get a good picture of that muscle group in your mind. Next, raise your arm and produce tension in that muscle group by making a tight fist and hold the tension for 10 seconds, paying close attention to the feelings of tension and tightness. Make it hard and tight. Then just let all of that tension drop out all at once as you release your arm. For the next 20 seconds, I would like you just to compare and contrast the feelings of relaxation with the feelings of tension that you were experiencing a moment ago. Now, once again I would like you to raise your arm and produce the tension and tightness in the first muscle group, the right forearm and hand, and hold that for 10 seconds. Hold that tension. Study the tension. And again just let all of the tension drop, refocusing now on the feelings of relaxation in that muscle group. Compare and contrast the feelings of relaxation with the tension that was there just a moment ago."

Sequentially, the process continues through the 16 muscle groups one at a time. Below is a list of the 16 muscle groups to focus on in the early stages of relaxation training.

1. Right forearm and hand
2. Right biceps
3. Left forearm and hand
4. Left biceps
5. Forehead
6. Upper cheeks and nose
7. Lower cheeks and mouth
8. Throat and neck
9. Chest and shoulders
10. Abdomen
11. Right thigh
12. Right calf
13. Right foot
14. Left thigh
15. Left calf
16. Left foot

It is generally preferable to review with individuals how specifically to produce tension in each muscle group before attempting the procedure. The following is a reminder of how best to produce tension in the various muscle groups. However, other methods are effective, and some people may prefer their own technique.

- Hands and forearms (right and left): Raise arm and make a tight fist.
- Biceps (right and left): Pull elbows in toward body with elbows bent.
- Forehead: Lift eyebrows as high as possible with eyes closed.
- Upper cheeks and nose: Squint the eyes and wrinkle the nose.
- Lower cheeks and mouth: With teeth together, pull corners of the mouth back.
- Neck and throat: Pull the chin downward while at the same time preventing it from actually touching the chest.
- Chest and shoulders: Take a deep breath, hold it, and pull the shoulder blades back and together.
- Abdomen: Tighten up the stomach as if bracing for a punch.
- Thighs (right and left): Tighten the thighs by lifting the leg off the chair while at the same time attempting to push it back down onto the chair.
- Calves: Point the toes toward the head.
- Feet: Curl the toes and turn the foot inward only until tension is experienced (to avoid cramping).

After completing the exercise, review with participants their experiences. Question how tension levels changed. Some may have negative reactions regarding the exercise - for example, discomfort, feelings of uneasiness, or loss of control. Discuss any concerns with participants and reassure them that anxiety and difficulty in focusing attention are common in early training.

The components to emphasize again should be the following.

1. Tension and relaxation are incompatible.
2. Relaxation training is a skill that can be learned and applied by the individual.
3. Relaxation methods must be practiced on a regular basis to be effective.

In programs that will last more than a day (e.g., 2-day workshop, week-long seminar), we strongly recommend that you go through the procedure on more than one occasion. This will reinforce the notion of practice and allow participants to begin to feel some of the benefits of relaxation. After teaching the basic components of this skill, you will want to help individuals with some practical elements, which include the following.

1. Establishing a good time for practicing.
2. Identifying a place for practicing (quiet, without distractions of telephone, children, etc.).
3. Setting up a way of monitoring their practice and level of relaxation achieved.
4. Using an audiotape.
5. Paying special attention to extra-tense areas.

Finally, it is important to remember that as relaxation training does produce bodily changes, persons with chronic medical problems should check with their physicians before beginning a regular practice routine. This is particularly important for insulin-dependent diabetics and people with hypertension.

The second form of relaxation to be discussed is an adaptation of Benson's (1975) relaxation response. Essentially, it is an abbreviated relaxation procedure that incorporates recall of the feelings of relaxation without producing the tension. Individuals are instructed to pay attention to their breathing and repeat the word "calm" or "relax" to themselves while exhaling. Tell them that with this technique they may find that they can eliminate the tension phase and just concentrate on relaxing each muscle group by recalling the feelings of relaxation they have learned to recognize. To do this, have participants close their eyes while lying comfortably in a reclining chair or or on bed. Describe the procedure as follows:

Focus on relaxing each part of your body in turn until your entire body is relaxed. Just "let go" of any tension that you notice in your body, relaxing to the best of your ability. After you have completely relaxed all the muscle groups of your body, shift your attention to your breathing. Notice how slow and regular it is. Breathe through your nose. As you exhale, say to yourself the word "calm." If your mind begins to wander, just focus on your breathing. (Continue for 15 minutes.) This allows you to associate the word "calm" with the feelings of relaxation. With practice, you should be able to repeat the word "calm" to yourself when you are feeling stressed or anxious to help reduce these feelings and thereby gain more control of the high stress situation. The benefits can include reduced blood pressure, heart rate, breathing rate, and muscle tension through the inhibition of your body's reactions to the fight-or-flight response reviewed earlier. After you have completed this, sit quietly for a few minutes and enjoy the pleasant feelings of relaxation. Slowly open your eyes and remain seated for a couple of minutes before standing up.

Success with this shortened version is important in progressing toward the goal of being able to relax upon command. With regular practice, relaxation skills allow people to monitor their tension levels throughout the day and reduce them as necessary. They should be encouraged periodically to assess their tension levels, if necessary through such reminders as a piece of red tape placed on a wristwatch. Encourage participants to practice their relaxation before a potentially stressful situation (e.g., talking with a difficult, demanding customer or patient or approaching a supervisor to discuss a problem) and reward themselves for increasing their self-control and coping skills.

AN ADDITIONAL BENEFIT
OF RELAXATION TRAINING

Members of many occupations, particularly law-enforcement and health-care personnel, are frequently subjected to angry, offensive, and insulting individuals. It is often necessary for them to control their own anger in order to maintain control and keep themselves task-focused. Calming an agitated person requires remaining calm yourself. One of the most important things one must do to control anger is to recognize the signs of arousal as soon as they occur. The relaxation exercises described will sharpen participants' skills so that they might better recognize some subtle physiological signs of stress. As individuals become more and more sharply tuned to the signs of tension and tightness, they will achieve a greater ability to short-circuit the anger process. Remind participants that as they learn to relax more easily, their ability to regulate anger will improve.

MODIFYING SELF-STATEMENTS

In this section, participants will learn the importance of the cognitive components of the stress response (things that they say to themselves), and how to challenge these "self-statements" when they are not appropriate and are contributing to their perception of stress. This component is based on the work of Ellis and Beck, among others. As with relaxation training, a good rationale should be included in your introduction to this part of the program. Elaborate on the fact that humans are thinking animals. As we move around and go about our daily routines, we continuously think about what we do. We have expectations about how something we do will come out. We have concerns, beliefs, judgments, and attitudes. The things we say to ourselves make up our inner speech or "self-statements," which can be compared to talking to yourself. Our reactions to stress are closely tied to self-statements.

An example will serve to point out how self-statements can influence our stress levels. Suggest the following scenario to participants to encourage their thinking about self-statements.

Imagine that you were asked to speak to a large group of citizens regarding the stress involved in your job. If you think to yourself, "I'm no good at giving talks" (a self-statement), chances are that stepping in front of such a group will be frightening. Your prejudgments regarding your capabilities partly determine your reaction to an event. Inner speech is also used to keep track of how we are doing and to rehearse in our heads what we plan to do. For example, in planning to drive from your home to the store, you might say to yourself, "The shortest route is up Fifth Street to Maple, then left. I need to watch out for that dangerous intersection in about a mile" (another self-statement). This type of self-talk guides us through the demands of everyday situations.

Let us look at another type of self-statement. Say two employees have just received criticism from their supervisor concerning a specific aspect of their job performance. Everyone periodically experiences disappointments and frustrations, but these two persons may react differently to this stressful event depending on their self-statements, or what they say to themselves about the event in relation to their self-concept. One person may say, "Well, I made a mistake this time, which reflects badly on my performance. I've done better before and I can do better next time." The other person may say something like, "I'm no good at this job, and I'll never perform in a manner that my supervisor approves of." Each of these persons is likely to think differently about himself or herself and the supervisor, but more important, their self-statements are likely to affect how they actually do in future job performance. The second employee may undergo considerable anxiety while attempting to perform the job in the hope of pleasing the supervisor. After continually making such negative self-statements as "I'm no good at doing that," it is possible to develop beliefs about oneself that are not accurate, for example, "I am a goof, and I can't do anything right." We may start to overgeneralize, beginning to believe what we say to ourselves about ourselves.

In the model of stress discussed earlier, we emphasized life events or stressors as the first step in the relationship between stress and disease, and then focused on the *perception* of the situation as the key to our reactions and responses. Self-statements represent our perception of the event (potential stressor). Discuss how negative self-statements can lead to the following problems:

1. *Overgeneralization.* Rather than confining thoughts and feelings to the specific situation, the person generalizes to other things. Common words in overgeneralized self-statements include always, never, and forever. Examples include: "This always happens to me" and "Things will never change." Overgeneralized self-statements serve as a prediction of the future and lead to feelings of helplessness.

2. *Catastrophizing.* In this case, the person thinks the worst. Rather than thinking that the stressor is unpleasant, the person views it as a tragedy. Common words in catastrophizing self-statements include horrible, incredibly awful, and tragic. Examples include: "This is the worst thing I could imagine" and "My life is ruined."

3. *Self-Pressure.* In self-pressured statements, one thinks about how one has not lived up to some standard (which is usually very vaguely defined).

Instead of thinking about what one *wants*, one thinks about how things *should* be. Common self-pressure words include should and must. Examples include: "I should never have let that happen," "I must get this done today," and "If I make a mistake, it means I'm inept."

4. *Black-or-White Thinking.* In this case, the individual emphasizes the extremes of situations while ignoring the "middle ground." Events are viewed as all bad or all good. Similarly, people are viewed as having all positive or all negative qualities. Examples include: "She is a really wonderful individual whom I adore, but I just despise *him*," "Going skiing for a week would be the best vacation I could ever imagine, but going fishing would be an absolute total drag," and "All tourists drive like idiots."

5. *Blaming.* Blaming occurs when a person seeks to blame someone else (or something else) when an unpleasant situation occurs. Common words include your fault. Examples include: "You should have known better" and "This is all his fault."

Have participants think of some specific life situations that they and most people would perceive of or interpret as stressful. Encourage them to begin with a general life situation (not necessarily specific to their job). To get participants thinking about this task, begin with a sample list of two life events - one traumatic and the other less traumatic, but irritating: (a) the unexpected death of a close family member and (b) oversleeping on a particularly important day of work.

Now have participants concentrate on what they believe are (or may have seen as) typical perceptions or what we have now called self-statements. Encourage them also to notice the possible behavioral and emotional reactions. Here is the example for the first two events (if you can think of other possible perceptions or reactions, add them):

Possible Situational Stressor	Some Possible Negative Self-Statements	Problems Arising from Self-Statements
Unexpected death of a family member	This is horrible. I can't believe it's happening. It's just not possible.	Overgeneralization

25

Possible Situational Stressor	Some Possible Negative Self-Statements	Problems Arising from Self-Statements
	His wife should have made him stop smoking.	Blaming
	I can't live without him.	Catastrophizing
Oversleeps on important day of work	Damn! I shouldn't have done this.	Self-pressure
	Nothing ever goes right for me.	Overgeneralization
	Since I can't be there on time, I might as well not go.	Black-or-white thinking

Now, for a stressor that participants have identified, have them list some possible negative self-statements and possible problems arising from such self-statements on a form such as below:

Stressor	Negative Self-Statements	Problem

For most participants, this exercise will be unlike anything they have done before, and so will be difficult at first. Reassure them that it takes practice to recognize our thoughts, especially our negative self-statements. However, it is apparent from these examples that negative self-statements need to be modified. To get rid of negative self-statements, we need to replace "faulty words" (e.g., always, never, should) with more specific words. We need to confine our thoughts to the specific stressor. Here are some challenges for the earlier examples to share with participants (encourage them to provide others):

EXAMPLE 1:
DEATH OF CLOSE FAMILY MEMBER

Negative Self-Statement	Challenge
This is horrible.	I am really sad that this happened.
His wife should have made him stop smoking.	I wish he could have stopped smoking as I worry that it may have contributed to his death.
I can't live without him.	I will really miss him.

EXAMPLE 2: OVERSLEEPING ON A
PARTICULARLY IMPORTANT DAY OF WORK

Negative Self-Statement	Challenge
Damn! I shouldn't have done this.	It is unfortunate that I overslept. I wish I had gotten up on time.
Nothing ever goes right for me.	Oversleeping today is something I'm irritated about.
Since I can't be there on time, I might as well not go.	Since I won't be there on time, I'll call and let them know I'll be late.

Now have participants write down some challenges for the negative self-statements that they identified earlier on a form such as seen on page 28.

Negative Self-Statement   Challenge

STRESS ANALYSIS

In this section, we concentrate on closely examining troublesome situations. By using the technique of stress analysis, individuals can learn how systematically to analyze a specific situation: how they felt and what they thought, how they contributed to the outcome, and what they liked and did not like about the outcome. By learning this skill, participants will become aware of their goals for certain situations and will have a much better chance of achieving the desired results. Point out that in learning stress analysis, participants will not be instructed in what to do, nor will it be an intensive therapy experience. Rather, it is a way of developing an effective strategy for understanding stressful situations and making some changes as needed.

The technique of stress analysis can be learned either on an individual basis or in a stress management group, but there are a few points that need to be mentioned to group participants. After some initial shyness, people are often glad to relate their experiences to others. You will find that many participants in your group share some of the same difficulties in areas related to work as well as their personal life. In conducting stress analysis in a group format, participants will be able to see how others might respond. Similarly, participants will have the opportunity to help others solve problems.

Stress analysis is based on the behavioral technique of functional analysis and the more specific technique of situational analysis developed by McCullough (1980).

Both analyses systematically identify and analyze different components of a particular problem. One common difficulty you will encounter in working with stressed individuals is their inability to identify what is stressful about a particular event. They may tell you how "stressed" (again in vague terms) they felt after being denied a job promotion, but they might not be able to specify what was most troublesome. Stress analysis helps them to break down the situation into different components, and also helps them to solve problems for future stress events. After learning the skill and applying this technique to different situations, the person will be able to:

1. More clearly define a stressful situation.
2. Identify thoughts that accompany the situation (particularly negative self-statements).
3. Identify physiological, emotional, and behavioral arousal cues.
4. See positive and negative consequences of behavior in a stressful situation.
5. Identify ways to handle similar stressful situations more effectively.

You will want to introduce this intervention technique by first explaining each of the six steps of stress analysis as follows:

1. *Describe the situation.* Tell where it happened, when, and who was involved. Give a clear beginning and ending. What did you do in the situation? How did it end?

   This first step gets the individual to define a discrete incident. For example, rather than the person's feeling stressed about his or her interactions with a spouse during the weekend, this step makes the person identify one specific component. It eliminates global perceptions and responses by introducing structure and focus.

2. *Describe your feelings.* Identify any arousal states - physiological or emotional. Look back to the "Stress Response Index" for examples.

   Here, the individual has to focus awareness on sensations and feelings. This helps the person to realize that there are certain cues that accompany stressful situations.

29

3. *Describe your self-statements.* Identify any thoughts that went through your mind. If you are unable to recall any specific thoughts, then make a guess at a likely thought. Common ones are "Why me?" and "Not again."

   As we mentioned before, the model of stress and illness emphasizes the cognitive component that accompanies the stressor - how the individual interprets the event. This step is very important as it helps to clarify the particular meaning of a situation. For example, a thought like "I really can't accomplish anything" following the failure of an important job assignment conveys the extraordinary importance of the situation (accomplishing this assignment means "I'm a worthwhile person"), as well as how much the individual may generalize.

4. *How did you want the situation to come out?* Given the situation, what were your goals for its outcome? What were you hoping to have happen?

   Our emphasis here is that people cannot get what they want if they do not know what it is that they want. Interestingly, people can often admit to a goal in retrospect (often not a particularly laudable one), but they may be unaware of their goals during the actual situation. For example, say that the telephone company screwed up your bill and in calling the company to try and straighten things out, you reach a rude and unhelpful person. The situation ends with your screaming at the person about the incompetency and inefficiency of the telephone company. In reviewing this situation, you can see that if the goal was to express frustration and anger, the goal was accomplished. Sometimes expression of feelings is a primary goal. On the other hand, if the goal was to get the person to help straighten out the billing problem, the actions taken certainly were not in line with the goal.

5. *What were the positive and negative parts of the outcome of the situation?*

   Although people can readily identify the negative consequences of their actions or of the situation (e.g., the telephone employee hung up on the call), they may have much more difficulty seeing any positive elements. We emphasize this part of the analysis to help them see that almost all situations have some beneficial outcomes. People find themselves in similar situations and may chastise themselves with, "Why do I keep getting myself in this same stupid situation? Didn't I learn from last time?" An individual may not have learned from a previous situation because there may be some reinforcers at work that actually encourage a repetition of the situation.

6. *In what ways would you have liked the situation to have turned out differently?*

This final step allows the person to specify a preferred outcome and begins the step of problem solving for next time - seeing that there is something that can be done differently next time.

WHICH SITUATIONS?

It is helpful to assist participants in choosing situations on which to practice stress analysis. Their events should be ones that involve interactions with other people and ones in which they felt somewhat dissatisfied or stressed. Offer some ways to help participants recall a few events that might be good examples for applying the stress analysis exercise.

1. Have them think back to the last time they raised their voices and regretted it.
2. Have them think back to the last time they were disappointed in their performance at work.
3. Have them think back to the last time they had to interact with another employee (or supervisor, patient, salesperson) who annoyed them.

These suggestions should get participants thinking. The examples need not be particularly personal or private. The important point is to choose real-life experiences that have happened to participants in the past so that they can learn this skill to apply to different kinds of situations. In reviewing situations, have participants rate them on a scale of 1 to 10. Let 1 represent the feeling of complete relaxation - not a worry on the mind or a tense muscle in the body. Let 10 represent an extremely unpleasant, uncomfortable anxiety and tension - a feeling of being all knotted up. Have participants examine situations that are

31

rated *5 and above.* After explaining the situation, we suggest that you go through an example of stress analysis. Share with participants a realistic stressful *real-life* situation, and verbally go through the six steps of stress analysis. We find it useful to provide yet another example of how this technique is done. Here is a typical situation that lends itself nicely to stress analysis. Describe the situation and how the technique was applied.

Example (Jim). "One of the most recent stressful situations that I can think of happened last Tuesday. I had a really bad day at work - I mean nothing went right that day. I had planned to work on the family car that evening as it had been acting up lately, and since I had plans for the other nights of the week, that was the only time I had. Anyway, after I finished supper I headed to the garage to start working. I walked toward where I keep my tool box (which I just got for Christmas). I couldn't believe it, the tool box was gone. My first thought was that it had been ripped off, but then I saw a note on the work table. 'Jim, I stopped by to borrow your socket wrench set but you weren't home. I'll bring it back later this evening, O.K.? - Bob.' Of course, it wasn't O.K. - this was the one night this week that I needed my tools and they were gone. Bob is one of my best friends, but I don't think I've ever been so angry at him. Couldn't he have waited until I got home to ask me? Did he have to take the whole box? I felt like I wanted to let him know how put off I was by what he did. Then I went inside the house and thought about whether I should call him, and if I did call, what I should say - but I couldn't even think straight. I ended up just sitting around the house and fuming for the next 2 hours. Around 9:00 p.m., Bob stopped by with the tool box. I didn't tell him how much he had inconvenienced me and how angry I was about it. I just said that the garage was going to be locked from now on and told him I was tired and didn't have time to talk anymore." (See Jim's Stress Analysis Form on p. 59.)

After going through an example such as the one above, have someone apply the technique to a specific situation. (See Stress Analysis Form on p. 60.)

EFFECTIVE COMMUNICATION SKILLS

The goal of this component is to help people communicate with others more effectively. The stress analysis is very helpful for identifying goals for situations and general ideas for changing outcome. By the time you get to the communications portion of the program, it should be readily apparent that most stressful situations identified by participants involved interpersonal elements. In this component of the program, awareness is very important. This component begins with helping the individual determine "How do I come across?" and moves to teaching some specific, practical skills.

SOME BASIC PRINCIPLES OF COMMUNICATION

We begin this section with a didactic presentation on communication, which is based on the work of Watzlawick, Beavin, and Jackson (1960). First, it is important to explain how pervasive communication is. Communication takes many forms. If we are in the presence of another person, we are communicating. We have no choice in such a situation - we cannot *not* communicate. This reflects our first principle of communication - *every interpersonal behavior is a communication.* Everything done in the presence of another person gives out a message. We can make choices regarding our actions, but no matter how hard we try, we cannot not communicate. Even the fact that we ignore another person is important information and communicates a message.

The second principle of communication is that *interpersonal behavior communicates at two levels - verbal and nonverbal.* The verbal component is the content. With the same content, two very different messages can be conveyed. To illustrate this, role-play two statements with identical content (say a request by a supervisor to attend a meeting) with different nonverbals. In one, use a loud, belligerent voice while staring intensely at a participant. In the other, use a normal tone of voice, smile as you make the request, and extend your hand to shake the participant's. Both examples convey the same message ("there is an important meeting that I want you to attend"), but although the messages may be the same, the *way* in which it is conveyed (nonverbal) carries very different meanings. An authoritarian air can be demonstrated through voice and gestures. The belligerent tone might be interpreted as, "I mean business." Perhaps the supervisor is angry or feels the individual neglected important meetings in the past and so, the importance of this particular meeting needs emphasis. All of these are possible explanations.

At times it is difficult to interpret exactly what is being conveyed besides the content of the message. This happens for two reasons:

1. Nonverbal messages and other "relationship" messages are much more difficult to interpret accurately than are verbal or content messages.
2. Often the nonverbal elements actually contradict the verbal (content) message.

Thus it is important that in your didactic presentation regarding communication you focus on nonverbal elements of communication. Specifically, we discuss the following five areas - for details, see Knapp (1978).

Physical Characteristics and Influencers. These include body physique, general appearance, weight, skin color, and the like. Influencers include clothing, cologne, hairpieces and hair styles, and so on.

Although physical characteristics may influence another person, we generally have little control over these features. However, by assessing our physical characteristics, we can be aware of how they influence others. For example, a person with a large heavy-set frame will appear more dominating and overpowering than someone of a smaller frame size. As an exercise, have members jot down a description of their own physical characteristics and what messages they might convey. In contrast to these physical characteristics over which we have little control, influencers are things that affect our appearance by our manipulation. Have members discuss the role of their own influencers - particularly if their job requires a uniform.

Body Motions. These include gestures, movements of arms and legs, facial expressions, posture, and eye contact.

The following meanings are conveyed by different body motions.

- "Open" body posture (arms/legs unfolded): friendliness, openness
- Steady eye gaze: intimidation
- Fiddling with keys/objects or finger tapping: anxiety, sense of urgency or "hurry up"

- Standing while another is sitting: dominance, one-upmanship
- Body leaning slightly forward: inviting interpersonal interaction
- Facing another squarely: welcoming communication; interest
- Tightly crossed arms and legs: closedness, defensiveness
- Looking away, lack of eye contact: disinterest, possibly anxiety

When discussing body motions, have participants identify the body motions they generally consider.

Vocal Qualities. Such qualities include rhythm, pitch, loudness, and tone. Some common connotations are as follows:

- Monotone: disinterest, boredom
- Loudness: increasing anger, hostility
- Fast rate: anxiety, enthusiasm
- Slow rate: depression
- Deep tone: harshness

Many individuals are not aware of their voice qualities until they listen to themselves on a tape recorder. Thus, we find using a tape recorder to be a good exercise to increase awareness. Have someone repeat the phrase "I wish you hadn't done that" three times - each time conveying a different message (anger, sadness, and empathy). Discuss differences in vocal qualities among the three.

Personal Space. By creating too much distance (more than 6 feet), distress is communicated. In the American culture, standing too close (less than 3 feet) conveys dominance and authority. It may induce anxiety or anger in the other party. To demonstrate the importance of personal space, try the following exercise for a group. Have participants pair up and stand almost nose to nose and instruct them to carry on a conversation for 2 minutes. Stop the conversation and have members freeze in their positions. Then ask them to attend to their body language. In most cases, you will find that the forced closeness has resulted in other distancing techniques (e.g., crossed arms, body shifts).

35

Behaviors. We often give out messages through our actions. For example, if we are late for an appointment, we may be communicating that we do not regard the person as important. Similarly, if someone calls us and leaves a message and we do not get back to the person, we may communicate that we are too busy to return the call.

VERBAL ELEMENTS AND
THE MESSAGES THEY MAY CONVEY

In addition to the nonverbal elements, verbal elements also provide certain messages. Certain verbal patterns can be barriers to communication. For example:

- Attributional statements, such as, "You make me so angry I could scream," elicit defensiveness and convey that others are responsible for our feelings. Take Jim who, in the earlier example of stress analysis, found his tool box missing from the garage. Among Jim's reactions when next seeing his friend Bob may have been such statements as, "You ruined my day off" or "Don't you have any consideration for other people's property?" These comments convey blame, anger, and distrust. In blaming Bob for "ruining his day," Jim is not taking any responsibility for his own reactions or feelings. In contrast, he could have used the technique of "owning one's feelings." By clearly stating his own feelings, blame could be avoided. For example, Jim could have said, "Bob, I'm really annoyed because I had planned to use my tools today and you didn't ask me before borrowing them." The use of "I" language takes responsibility for personal feelings and can reduce defensiveness in the other person. When you explain the "I language" to participants, it is important to emphasize that no one can *make* us feel a certain way.
- Interruptions convey disrespect, disinterest.
- Verbal hurry ups ("Uh-huh, uh-huh," "Get to the point") convey "I don't have time for this."
- Commands convey "I'm in charge," " You're not worth some courtesy," " I'm in a hurry."
- Frequent questioning directs the conversation and may communicate too much attention to the content.
- Encouragement ("Go on," "I see") communicates interest, attention.

- Open-ended questions (ones that cannot be answered Yes or No) show "I care about what you think. I don't have a preconceived notion of the 'right' answer."
- Silence communicates "I'm not going to communicate directly with you right now" or "I'm thinking (but I want to make you uncomfortable in the process)."

IMPROVING PERSONAL COMMUNICATION SKILLS

There are several active communication skills that you can teach that will help individuals improve their interactions. The three skills to focus on are reflections, paraphrasing, and pinpointing.

Reflections. Reflections involve listening carefully to a speaker and mirroring back to the speaker what you hear being said as you emphasize the speaker's feelings or emotions. For example:

Rich: "Damn, I'm frustrated. I really thought I did well on that promotions test. Guess I'll have to try it again next year."

Tom: "Sounds like you thought you had done well on the test and you're really frustrated."

Tom has listened to what Rich was saying. He is not attempting to interpret what has been said, but merely to reflect what has been said. Although reflecting may initially seem like simply "parroting," this skill communicates listening and understanding, and invites further communication. Encourage individuals not to be in a hurry to give advice or suggestions. Listening and understanding should always precede advice and recommendations. Using reflections communicates that the listener recognizes the feelings the other person is expressing.

Paraphrasing. In contrast to reflections, which involve mirroring, paraphrasing involves briefly restating the content of a speaker's message in similar words.

Essentially it means determining "where the speaker is coming from" and does require some "interpretation." For example:

Susan: "I've been thinking about finding another job. It's not that I don't like what I'm doing, it's just that

I'm bored with doing the same thing all of the time. Sometimes I wonder whether there isn't something available somewhere that would be more exciting and challenging."

David: "You like your work but think you are sort of in a rut and could stand a change."

David summarized the gist of what Susan was saying. He did it briefly and with similar words, but without "parroting" word for word. Paraphrasing may seem awkward at first, but it is a very effective communication tool and is used much more often than we realize. It is particularly useful for reducing misunderstandings in communication.

Pinpointing. This is another technique to enhance understanding and improve communication. Essentially, pinpointing involves requesting speakers to elaborate on something they have said that is unclear to you. "Could you give me an example?" and "Could you be more specific?" are two examples of pinpointing. Pinpointing encourages speakers to continue and clarify the content of what they are saying. It is particularly useful when interacting with individuals who are expressing global feelings of distress, but are having difficulty describing the details of their situation. For example:

Mike: "Man, what a week this has been. I really don't know if I could handle another one like this."

Jane: "What went on to make this such a bad week?"

One characteristic of being under a lot of stress is feeling overwhelmed and unable to express specifically what has been happening to make us feel the way we do. Jane sensed that Mike was feeling stressed and assisted him in pinpointing the sources of his stress by asking for details. In doing so, she increased her understanding of what was contributing to Mike's stress. By pinpointing the source of his difficulties, Mike is more likely to identify potential solutions to his problems.

USEFULNESS OF ROLE-PLAYING

After describing each of these techniques, it is helpful to have individuals role-play situations in which they can try them out. Two good examples of role-play situations are (a) a co-worker complaining about the boss, and (b) someone providing evaluation to a subordinate (appropriate for individuals in supervisory positions).

We have found that videotaping and playback of these role-plays can be extremely useful. After role-playing a situation, have the participants critique it. Then play back the video and solicit feedback from everyone by prompting with questions about verbal and nonverbal behaviors.

Verbal Behaviors

- Was the statement of the main idea direct and to the point?
- Were the statements firm but not hostile? (Used in cases of giving negative feedback.)
- Did the statement show some consideration, respect, or recognition of the other person?
- Did the statement blame the other person for the speaker's feelings?
- What kind of statements were used (paraphrases, reflections, etc.)?

Nonverbal Behaviors

- Was eye contact present?
- Was the speaker's voice level appropriate?
- Did the speaker look confident?
- Was the statement "flat" or expressive?
- Was the body posture open?
- Did the voice vary in tone?

PROBLEMS IN COMMUNICATION: GAMES AND DIFFICULT PEOPLE

The key problem in communication arises when one person does not know or understand what the other person is trying to say or when we feel we cannot communicate with certain "difficult" people. In 1967, Eric Berne described many different games in his book *Games People Play*. Two common games are "*Yes, but . . .*" and "*Questions but no answers.*"

"**Yes, but . . .** In the "yes, but . . ." game, the person responds verbally as though agreeing but qualifies every agreement with a "yes, but." Essentially, the person is

39

communicating, "I don't agree with you," but is avoiding outright confrontation by appearing to agree. For example:

John: "You know, I'm really getting tired of making excuses to the supervisor about why you're late every Friday morning."

Fred: "Yes, I know you're right. But just try to understand that Thursday nights are my softball games. For the past 2 weeks we've had doubleheaders. I get home after 11:00 p.m., then by the time I grab a snack and unwind, it's midnight by the time I get to sleep. You can see why I'm dragging."

John: "I know it's tough to get up on time when you stay out late. But the rest of us manage and I'm in an awkward position having to make excuses for you, Fred."

Fred: "Yes, I know you are, but it won't be like this for much longer. You see, we shouldn't have many more doubleheaders."

John: "I'm not sure that you're hearing me. I don't want to cover anymore. I want you to take responsibility."

Fred: "Yeah, John, but . . . ." (Fred responds with a "yes, but . . ." to everything John says.)

Questions but no answers. This game is a way of appearing to be engaged and interested while actually inducing conflict. Its most common form is to ask a question that the listener is really not free to answer. For example, a wife might say to her husband, "Do you really want to go bowling with your friends for the second night this week?" Is the wife asking for information? Obviously there is a "correct" answer that she is expecting. Two messages are being communicated: "Do you want . . .?" (information question) and "I don't want you to . . ." (statement of own feelings).

There are two reasons for playing this type of game. First, the wife may not be fully aware of her own feelings, so she is unable to express them honestly. Second, she may fear direct expression of her feelings so she expresses them indirectly.

How can one intercede in this or other games? Both participants can change their pattern. The game player can ask, "What do I feel?" "What do I want to communicate and how can I communicate my feelings in a non-threatening manner?" (*Hint*: Use *I* language).

When interacting with a game player, one needs to ask, "What is the message this person wishes to communicate?" In some situations, it may be effective to confront the person on the game. However, it is important to remember that the game may not be intentional or deliberate. Consequently, it is very important to avoid accusations and other negative reactions. For example, in the earlier situation regarding bowling, the husband might respond, "You're asking if I want to go bowling again. Well, to be honest, I really enjoy bowling. I had so much fun last time with the guys, I'm eager to go again. But I'm wondering if you want to know something else, or perhaps you're trying to say you would prefer I not go." In this communication, the husband has utilized paraphrasing and *I* statements. In addition, he has honestly stated his own feelings. He has avoided accusations, but he has gently confronted his wife by pointing out what her intention may be.

Difficult People: Idiots and Jerks (A-Holes). While members will listen to the general idea of problems that occur in communicating and may be able to identify some examples where game playing occurs, you will see much more animated discussion when you bring up the topic of difficult people and those to whom we refer as "idiots" and "jerks" (or a-holes). Begin by having individuals define these labels and give examples of situations in which they have had to deal with such individuals. Be sure to include nonverbal characteristics associated with these types.

Idiots say and do things that make no sense. An idiot is the person on your baseball team who, with three balls, no strikes, and the bases loaded (score 10 to 9 in the bottom of the ninth inning), goes after a bad ball, causes the last out, and the team loses a game.

Idiots make mistakes like this generally because they have not learned different responses. At other times, their minds are on other things (perhaps problems), and in failing to attend to what is at hand, they make idiotic mistakes.

Jerks also do illogical things, but they seem to know it. They act as though they do not care if they are illogical. Unfortunately, there may also be verbal (or nonverbal) gestures of hostility and intimidation. A jerk

41

is the person in front of you in the cash-only, 10-item checkout line at the supermarket who, when the cashier totals the cost of his 20 items, hands her his credit card. When told that he must pay cash, he complains loudly and insists on seeing the manager.

REHEARSING AND ROLE-PLAYING

At this point, with lively discussion and involvement, you may wish again to use role-play with the video camera. After a few role-plays have been completed, have members discuss the verbal and nonverbal elements of the communication style. Replay the video and have them make additional comments on features they may have missed the first time. As the members discuss and act out examples of "difficult people," the point is not necessarily to come up with a well-defined system of difficult people, but to emphasize that there are several different types of people who are not easy to deal with and with whom we need to use new communication strategies. The differentiation of the label itself (jerk vs. idiot) is not important, but the use of such labels does mean, "I'm angry that this person is not doing what I would like."

Even the best communication effort may not produce positive results with certain people. Thus, it is important to help individuals evaluate and reflect upon whether they are satisfied with their own responses. In other words, was the message communicated as best it could be? It is not an easy task to handle these people. A natural response is frustration and anger. In helping people learn to deal with difficult people, you want to help them to focus on detaching themselves from their emotional reactions. This can be accomplished by applying the following five steps when dealing with a difficult person.

1. Ask yourself, "What verbal/nonverbal behaviors do I see?"
2. Then think, "What might this person be trying to communicate to me?" By focusing and attempting to understand the message, you can calm your emotional reaction (e.g., anger and frustration).

   Common messages: I'm scared. I'm confused. I want to appear powerful and in control. Help me. Go away. I've got something on my mind.

3. Ask yourself, "What do I want to come out of this interaction?" Note that whether the person is an idiot or a jerk is irrelevant. Both of these difficult people are failing to do things "your way." Stop labeling - there is no need to dwell on their shortcomings.
4. Ask yourself, "How can *I* communicate my message to the individual?" (both verbally and nonverbally).
5. Then *action.*

As with stress analysis, it is important to have participants apply these steps to a particular interaction. The following example is one we use to illustrate this technique for law enforcement officers.

An officer walks up to a car that he has just pulled over. Quickly getting out of his car, the motorist's first comments to the officer are, "Don't you have anything better to do than stop people for trivial offenses? Why don't you go find some real crime to fight?" Obviously, this man will be hard to handle, and the officer's natural responses are likely to be frustration, anger, or anxiety. The officer could apply the steps in this way.

1. *What verbal/nonverbal behaviors do I see?* The person jumped out of his car when I pulled him over, his voice was loud, he was staring at me, he was gesturing to me with his hands, he was shaking his head as if to say "No way."
2. *What might this person be trying to communicate to me?* Maybe the man has had a really bad day, maybe he is upset because his insurance is going to go up now, maybe he was robbed once and there weren't any police officers around to assist him, maybe he got another ticket recently and he's worried about losing his license. There are many possibilities for why he is acting the way he is.
3. *What do I want to come out of this situation?* I want to avoid conflict and to help this person understand why I pulled him over. I did not pull him over so I could get into a fight; all I want to do is enforce the traffic ordinances. There is no need to argue with him over my job responsibilities.
4. *How can I communicate my message to the individual?* First of all, I need to remain calm and not get upset. By staying calm and in control, I'll more ef-

fectively communicate to this person why I pulled him over. I'll acknowledge that I hear how upset he is, and I'll inform him clearly of my reasons for pulling him over. I'll avoid further blocking of communication by not interrupting the person or calling him names.

5. Then *action.* "I understand that you are upset because I pulled you over, however, it is important for you to understand my reasons for doing so. The speed limit in this area is 55 and I clocked you on radar at 69. Although I understand that tickets are costly, and that there are many things that you would rather be doing at this moment than getting a ticket, I am going to write you a citation for your violation."

Have people provide other situations and have them work out the application of the five steps. Brainstorm for specific ways to communicate nonverbally and how best to phrase their messages. Most likely, members will come up with strategies that you have presented earlier (finding something to reinforce, paraphrasing, etc.).

CHANGING LIFE-STYLE BEHAVIORS

We begin this component of our intervention strategies with some didactic information about the potential negative consequences of certain health-related behaviors. Specifically, we focus on smoking, obesity, poor eating habits, and lack of regular exercise. Patterns of disease in the United States have changed dramatically over the past 100 years, with an increase in what have been called the "preventable" disorders, including heart disease, cancer, and drug abuse. The role of behavioral factors in the incidence of these diseases has been widely reported in the scientific and lay press. "Scare tactics" are now considered neither necessary nor sufficient to change health-related behaviors, so we encourage you to present this information in a straightforward manner and to provide scientific evidence as appropriate.

The first part of your didactic emphasizes some specific health consequences associated with certain life-style behaviors. The American Cancer Society and the American Heart Association provide readily available, up-to-date statistics that you should share with participants. This information includes such findings as:

1. Heart diseases remain the leading cause of death in the United States, followed by cancer, cerebrovascular diseases, and accidents. In 1985, nearly one million Americans died from heart diseases and over 450,000 died from cancer.
2. Twenty-five percent of all cancer deaths and a large number of deaths from heart attack could be avoided by modifying just one behavior - smoking.
3. Overall, it is estimated that 50% of the deaths from the 10 leading causes of death in this country are attributable to modifiable life-style behaviors (Centers for Disease Control, 1980).
4. In 1988, the American Cancer Society reported that for males, the most common cancers are those of the lung, prostate, and colon/rectum. Among females, cancers of the breast, colon/rectum, and lung are most common. Lung cancer, however, is projected to be the leading cancer killer of both sexes in 1988, recently exceeding breast cancer as the major killer of females.
5. Smokers have more than twice the risk of heart attack as nonsmokers and two to four times the risk of sudden cardiac death when compared with nonsmokers. Smokers are also more likely to die from a heart attack.
6. Approximately 30% of all cancer is smoking related.
7. Estimates are that 30% to 40% of the over 500,000 deaths from coronary heart disease each year can be attributed to cigarette smoking.

People who continue to smoke are probably very aware of the potential health risks. In further discussion of negative health-related behaviors, we recommend that you emphasize "wellness" by describing how participants' lives could be improved as a result of risk-factor modification. Cite data, for example, showing that smoking cessation by one-pack-per-day smokers leads to dramatic reductions in risks of stroke and heart disease to levels approximating those of nonsmokers after approximately 10 years of cessation. Many factors have been identified that are thought to contribute to a decrease in the chances of developing cancer, including avoiding obesity; cutting down on total fat intake; eating more high-fiber foods, including foods rich in vitamins A and C; including cruciferous vegetables in the diet (e.g., cabbage, broccoli, cauliflower); cutting down on the consumption of salt-cured, smoked, and nitrite-cured foods; getting regular exercise; avoiding overexposure to the sun; and keeping alcohol consumption moderate. Recently, scientists have reported that for every 1% decrease in serum cholesterol, there is a corresponding 2% reduction in the risk of coronary heart disease. A 10% weight reduction among men aged 35 to 55 would produce an estimated 20% decrease in coronary heart disease (Ashley & Kannel, 1974). There is also evidence that men who lowered their cholesterol levels with diet and medication had fewer heart attacks and less heart disease than those who did not.

For those persons who are interested in learning stress management techniques and yet continue to consume caffeinated coffee or smoke cigarettes, a didactic on the effects of caffeine and nicotine may be in order. Point out that caffeine is a mild stimulant of the central nervous system, and as such has short-lasting but demonstrated effects on the cardiovascular system, including increases in blood pressure, heart rate, cardiac output, and stroke volume. It also serves to increase muscle tension, intestinal motility, and secretion of acid in the stomach. While enjoyed for its ability to increase our levels of alertness and concentration, too much caffeine probably decreases our ability to concentrate and may have an adverse effect on reaction time. Likewise, nicotine is a stimulant (and a natural poison if taken in sufficient quantity) that has the capacity to raise heart rate and blood pressure.

A great deal of this information will be new to participants, and as a result you may see many targeting changes in smoking or eating habits.

Now return to the stress-illness model and discuss how health-related behaviors relate to stress and potential physiological, emotional, or behavioral consequences. Consider the example of overeating in response to stress. Say an individual has an argument with a co-worker. She leaves the office irritable and upset, and passes the candy machine in the corridor. Her first perception of the event (self-statement) might be, "That Mark really irritates me. He is such a jerk." Then, "Nothing has gone right for me today. To heck with the diet, I really deserve a treat." The behavior that follows will be buying and eating a large package of candy. Later, emotional responses might be guilt and irritation. The physiological responses include the eventual lack of weight loss.

Another example is drinking too much alcohol as an attempt to unwind after a rough day. This can serve later to disrupt the sleep cycle. The next day, a resulting stressor may be oversleeping, awakening not feeling rested, or feeling "hung over." A possible perception (as the person wakes up) may be, "Oh no! I'll be late for work." Possible behavioral and emotional responses include hurrying to get ready, skipping breakfast, snapping at a spouse for not waking the person up, a day of feeling fuzzy and hassled at work, working less efficiently than usual, or even calling in sick.

In describing how health-related behaviors can be related to stress and illness, include how they can be a *response* to stressors. For example, many smokers and overeaters report that they smoke or eat more when they are feeling stressed and that such behaviors help them to relax. In the short run, they may actually feel better after smoking a cigarette or devouring a large banana split. The problem is that, in the long run, repeatedly engaging in such behaviors in response to stress (or failing to engage in certain healthful behaviors such as exercising) may reduce the body's ability to meet certain demands. The analogy is that just as your body must be healthy and strong to prevent infection and fight off germs to which you are exposed daily, so, too, must your body be strong to fight off the adverse effects of stress. A person who smokes lightly or not at all or a person who rarely or never drinks is less likely than the heavy smoker or drinker to develop the medical conditions associated with stress. Persons who are physically conditioned, when exposed to a stressful life event, show the usual fight-or-flight response; however, they "recover" or come back down to normal levels of heart rate and blood pressure more quickly, with fewer adverse effects on their bodies. Mention that these behaviors are also related to stress in a way having to do with our feelings of self-esteem and self-control. For example, all of us have made promises to ourselves to change certain behaviors (e.g., to quit smoking). Few of us are successful initially, however, and we may feel as if we have no control over our behavior. The result often is that we are angry and disappointed with ourselves, and we have lowered our self-esteem.

The purpose of the next section is to describe several techniques that can be useful in helping people make changes in these behaviors. Impress upon participants that ultimately they *do* have control over these behaviors, once they decide that the long-term benefits of changing health-related behaviors (e.g., improved health, improved self-esteem, better tolerance of stress, and actually reduced stress) are worth it.

GUIDELINES TO HELP ESTABLISH BEHAVIOR-CHANGE PROGRAMS

Basic behavioral principles provide the foundation for a behavioral self-management program targeting health-related behaviors. It is important to review these with persons who are considering implementing a program to change a certain behavior. Following is a list of basic behavioral principles we believe are important to review with participants. You should also briefly explain how they are relevant to modifying specific behaviors.

1. *All behaviors are learned and thus can be unlearned.* This means, for example, that one is not "destined" to overeat. As a facilitator, emphasize that troublesome behaviors have been learned; they are habits and all habits can be changed.
2. *Rewards are more effective than punishment.* While the empirical evidence is quite clear that it is better to reward (reinforce) a desired behavior than to punish an undesired behavior, people often have a hard time applying this principle. For example, a man may scold his 7-year-old son for not adhering to his 9:00 p.m. bedtime, but fail to reinforce him verbally when he does go to bed without prompting at or before his scheduled bedtime. It is very important that people reward themselves for changes in their behaviors. This leads to the third principle.
3. *Behavior that is reinforced tends to be repeated.* Thus, it is important for people to establish a system for rewarding themselves. However, reinforcement must continue. If a person has established a system of putting aside $2 each week toward a favorite record album as a reward for staying with a diet and then suddenly abandons the reward system (without replacing it), behavior change is less likely to be maintained.
4. *Rewards should follow the behavior as soon as possible.* This means that frequent short-term rewards

will be more effective than a delayed reward system. Weekly or daily rewards for adhering to a diet will be much more effective than a big reward at the end of the month.

The first step in producing a change in any health-related behavior involves identifying the target behavior that is to be changed (e.g., smoking, being overweight, drinking too much alcohol, not exercising). The targeted problem must be identified in terms of measurable behavior. A goal of "becoming thinner" is not a measurable behavior; losing 10 pounds is. It is important that the individual be specific. For example, if the goal is improving physical fitness, the goal might be operationalized in terms of minutes jogged during three exercise sessions each week, or a certain number of laps to swim in the pool. Emphasize that by being specific and measurable, it will make it easier to evaluate progress toward the goal.

Identifying the target behavior is generally easy. But why is it that if changing health-related behaviors has so many positive results, we have such a hard time following through? If you ask someone to think back to the last time he or she realized the necessity to lose a few pounds, to quit smoking, or to start exercising regularly, chances are the person can offer several excuses for not having followed through on changing the behavior. This brings us to another important part of modifying a behavior - identifying the potential barriers. Some people do not exercise regularly because they believe it takes too much time, interferes with work, causes pain, or requires equipment that they do not own or cannot afford. Others do not diet because they do not have support from other family members, or feel inconvenienced at having to prepare special meals. As we usually learn from our past mistakes, it is helpful to review past failures and to analyze the barriers that prevented the person from reaching the desired goal.

Before helping an individual to target a behavior and design a program, it is helpful to review some techniques for producing change.

Self-Monitoring. A good technique to start with is self-monitoring. This is simply a method of observing and recording behavior. For example, a smoker might self-monitor the number of cigarettes he or she smokes. Many smoking cessation programs encourage their members to carry an index card, which is divided up into the hours of the day. Each time the person smokes a cigarette, a check mark is made on the card corresponding to the time of day that the cigarette was smoked. In this way, the person can keep track of how many cigarettes were smoked and when, thus increasing awareness. Self-monitoring can sometimes help change a behavior just by making the person aware of how often he or she engages in a behavior. Self-monitoring is useful in determining a baseline or starting point.

Another form of self-monitoring is the use of a chart or goal thermometer. For example, if the goal is to lose 10 pounds, a chart or graph might be taped to the refrigerator. Each week at the same time of day, one would weigh oneself and record the weight on the graph for that week. A goal thermometer could be divided into 10 equally spaced, 1-pound segments. Each time one comes closer to one's goal (the top of the thermometer), one simply colors in the amount of weight loss. By keeping the graphs and goal thermometer in open view, others can also note one's progress, and offer support and encouragement.

Controlling Triggers. It has long been known that events that occur in our environment partially determine how we behave. Seeing brake lights illuminated on the car ahead when driving down the road signals a driver to slow down. Some behaviors seem more likely to take place under certain circumstances. Particular times, locations, or individuals are associated with certain behaviors and are called "triggers." For example, many people report that they most frequently smoke a cigarette after a meal or while enjoying a cup of coffee. Some people find themselves snacking each time they watch television. Once a person can identify those environmental events or triggers that are most often associated with a target behavior, specific self-help/self-control strategies can be employed to help modify the behavior. For example, the frequent snacker might snack in a variety of locations, including in front of the television set, in the car, in bed, in the den, or in a favorite chair while reading the paper. One strategy is to limit the target behavior to a restricted number of environments, or even to only one environment. Thus, a frequent snacker might restrict snacking to the kitchen as one attempt to gain control over the undesirable behavior. By identi-

fying triggers and actively intervening, the strong association between the behavior and the trigger (or stimulus)
can be broken.

Another strategy involves avoidance of high-risk
environments. A smoker who identifies being most likely
to smoke when with a group of people drinking coffee
may temporarily avoid this high risk environment as an
attempt to gain control over the smoking behavior. Another alternative is to engage in a different behavior when
the trigger occurs. For example, a person who overeats in
response to feelings of anxiety might engage in a brief
physical activity when anxious feelings arise (e.g., do 5 or
10 push-ups). Very heavy smokers can make an effort to
increase the length of time between each cigarette, slowly
but gradually working toward quitting. Together, these
techniques are referred to as stimulus control and have
been used extensively and successfully to help people
modify health-related behaviors.

Contracting. Many people have tried a contracting
strategy to change behavior, particularly with children.
For example, a parent might offer, "*If* you finish all of
the yard work, *then* you can play." When people self-
contract, they agree to reward themselves for engaging in
a particular behavior (such as exercising for 30 minutes)
or not engaging in a behavior (not smoking for an hour).
Once the base rate of a particular behavior has been
determined (through self-monitoring), a specific contract
can be developed. The type of rewards that will be utilized is important. Different people find different things
rewarding. Use of instruments such as the Reinforcement
Survey Schedule (Cautela & Kastenbaum, 1967) can help
in identifying a person's potential reinforcers. It is important to emphasize a basic rule of psychology - if a behavior is rewarded, it is more likely to be repeated. Rewards
can be *social* or *material*. Social rewards are such things
as being complimented in doing a good job, encouragement, and even a smile. Material rewards are things like
money, buying a special treat, going to a movie, and so
on.

There are a few guidelines to review when explaining
self-contracting as a method of changing health-related
behaviors. One is that it is important to break down a
larger goal into a number of small steps. For example, if
a person's target was to lose 10 pounds, the first goal
might be to stick to a 1,500-calorie-per-day diet for 1

week, and then to maintain a 1,200-calorie-per-day diet for 2 weeks. Once the goals have been specified and broken down into specific components and specific rewards have been identified, a contract that specifies the conditions can be written. For example, "*If* I stick to my 1,500-calorie-per-day diet for 1 week, *then* I will reward myself by buying new jogging shoes." (Avoid using food for a reward, of course!) In this way, each reward will be tied to each step toward the goal and the conditions are spelled out. The contract should be fair; that is, the terms should not be so difficult that they are unlikely to be met, or so easy that the contract is not challenging. In the case of dieting, we encourage using the goal of maintaining a specific diet rather than losing a number of pounds. Building gradual steps into contracts can help us experience success at several levels of increasing difficulty, thus minimizing the unpleasantness experienced when we try to do too much all at once. It can be helpful to set up weekly goals so that the target goal is accomplished gradually.

The individual can also contract with significant others. This form of contract is identical to a self-contract with one important addition. When a person contracts with significant others, not only are the conditions of the contract written down, but there is also a public commitment. A significant other might be a spouse, a friend, or a roommate. For example, a person might specify a jogging program with the first goal being to jog 20 minutes a day for 3 days a week. If this goal is accomplished, the reward might be to see a new movie. The contract can be set up describing these details, and shown to a significant other. Goals are discussed with this person, and then *both sign* it if the contract is found to be reasonable and fair. Once a week or so, the individual's progress is reported to the significant other. This can be a very useful technique to maintain motivation and enthusiasm toward achieving one's ultimate goal.

STRATEGIES FOR INCREASING SOCIAL SUPPORT

Much has been written about the usefulness of social support for behavior change. However, individuals are often reluctant to share their plans to change a certain behavior. They may fear ridicule if their plans should fail, or simply be reluctant to share the fact that they are having to employ techniques to assist them in changing when they should be able to rely on will power. First, encourage participants to identify individuals with whom they have frequent contact and who are influential in their lives. Such persons can fall into categories of helpful, sharing, harmful, and neutral. A helpful individual recognizes that you are trying to change a behavior and willingly offers specific advice and help. A sharing individual participates in efforts to change behavior (e.g., goes with you to the health club to work out). A harmful individual can intentionally or unintentionally sabotage behavior change (e.g., offers the dieter a high-calorie dessert). Neutral individuals do not help or harm behavior change; they simply do not care. After participants have identified these people, you will want to discuss the following strategies for increasing helpful support.

1. Ask for advice. "I heard that you recently quit smoking. I've tried three times, but always go back to it. What did you find was helpful to do when you had a craving for a cigarette?"
2. Obtaining a partner. "I often see you working out at the club when I'm there. I think it would helpful it we worked out together on a regular schedule so that we could encourage each other."
3. Being assertive in resisting harmful comments. "I appreciate the offer. I know you take pride in your desserts, but, as I mentioned before, I am trying to lose weight and I would really appreciate your support in helping me to cut down on sweets."
4. Informing others of your progress toward your goals. "I'm really excited about my new weight-loss program. I've lost 7 pounds this month."

Dealing with Barriers. Whereas one may be able to develop a contract like the ones described, it is often more difficult actually to implement it because of barriers. One's commitment to changing health-related behaviors helps determine how one faces and overcomes barriers. Before beginning a behavior change program, people need to identify potential barriers. Common weight-loss barriers include eating out on special occasions, the inconvenience of preparing "diet" foods, and the difficulty of refusing tempting foods that co-workers might bring into the office. Common exercise barriers include not having enough time, inclement weather, and equipment/health club expense. Among common smoking cessation barriers are working near other smokers, potential weight gain, and difficulty in resisting urges in social situations. After identifying barriers, individuals will need to troubleshoot specific solutions. For example, if a person complains about not having enough time to devote to an exercise program, a flexible program will have to be developed (e.g., exercise 10 minutes a day, six times per week, as opposed to 30 minutes a day, three times per week).

After reviewing the techniques, you can help participants develop individual programs by following these steps.

1. Clearly define the behavior to be addressed and the goal to be accomplished. *Example*: Improve aerobic fitness by jogging 2 miles three times per week.
2. Identify potential barriers and troubleshoot for solutions. *Example*: Barrier 1: "I'm too tired when I get home from work." Barrier 2: "I really can't afford the time." To overcome barrier 1: "I'll go to bed earlier at night." To overcome Barrier 2: "I'll build jogging into a regular routine."
3. Obtain a baseline in order to identify a current pattern of behavior. *Example*: Record how often you engage in jogging (and perhaps general physical activities).
4. Specify techniques that will be used to accomplish goals. *Example*: "My goal is to jog 2 miles at least three times each week. I will begin with jogging one-half mile three times a week and each week increase this by one-half mile. In 4 weeks I should be able to meet this goal. I will mark on my calendar each time I jog (self-monitoring). Each week that I meet my goal for that week, I will set aside $2 (small reward). At the end of 3 months, if I keep to my plan, I will have enough money to reward myself with that new bowling ball I've wanted (big reward)."

Four Steps Toward Life-Style Change

1. My target behavior to change: _____
_____.

2. I might run into some barriers in trying to make this change. For example, _____ might be a barrier.
   To overcome this barrier, I'll _____
   _____.

3. Next, I will keep a record of my typical pattern before starting my program. For the next _____ days, I will write down how often I _____.

4. To accomplish my goal, I will use the following technique(s): _____.

SEEKING PROFESSIONAL HELP

As mentioned earlier, you may encounter participants who appear to be experiencing difficulties for which stress management techniques may not be adequate. The best message to convey throughout the program is: "Generally, these techniques will work to help you decrease your current level of stress. However, if you find that problems persist, there are many other avenues to pursue. If you are serious about improving your life and being happier, don't stop if one potential solution is not enough."

The concept of counseling should be normalized with numerous such references throughout. We encourage you to share your own counseling experiences and those of other (anonymous) individuals who have benefited (despite initial reservations). Of course, it is important to be able to translate this into practical action, which means knowing who the credible counseling referrals are in the participants' communities. Contact local community mental health centers, private practitioners, pastoral counselors (located in many churches), and ask the following questions: With what kinds of client populations have you worked? What kinds of problems are typical to your clients (e.g., occupational stress, alcohol or other drug abuse, marital difficulties, depression)? What are your professional qualifications and training? What do you charge? Are your services reimbursable by most insurance carriers? Do you offer a sliding fee scale based on the client's ability to pay?

It is important to be able to provide some basic information about options for professional help when conducting stress groups or seminars. In discussing professional counseling, you will want to talk about the different types of interventions and professional resources that are available. It is also helpful to discuss with individuals what issues they may wish to clarify when seeking professional assistance. Begin your didactic by answering the following question.

WHO PROVIDES COUNSELING SERVICES?

Psychologists, psychiatrists, social workers, psychiatric nurses, pastors, and marital counselors are among the professionals most commonly providing counseling for stress-related difficulties. Their training and areas of expertise vary widely. Psychologists usually have doctoral degrees (PhD, EdD, or PsyD) in psychology. Most have completed an extensive program of education and an internship and have had supervisory experiences that have prepared them for licensure. However, licensing laws vary from state to state. It is important to emphasize that psychologists (unlike psychiatrists) cannot prescribe medications. Many lay people are confused about the difference between psychologists and psychiatrists. Thus, you will want to explain that psychiatrists are persons who have received a medical degree (MD) and usually have completed a residency in psychiatry. Psychiatrists who are board certified have also had 2 additional years of experience after their residency and have passed a special written exam.

Psychiatric social workers have a college degree plus at least 2 years of graduate training in a program accredited by the Council on Social Work Education. In addition, to be licensed, a psychiatric social worker must pass a written exam; licensing procedures vary from state to state. Psychiatric nurses are licensed registered nurses (RNs) with additional training and experience with emotional or behavioral disorders. Often, psychiatric nurses are affiliated with hospitals and may work within a group of mental health professionals that includes psychiatrists and psychologists. Pastoral counselors are ministers with specialized training in counseling, usually a master's degree. Visits often can be arranged through local churches, or in larger cities, at pastoral counseling centers. Marital counselors can be psychiatrists, psychologists, social workers, psychiatric nurses, or pastors with special training and licensure in the area of marital therapy.

In addition to these mental health professionals, there are often other sources of assistance in the community. Self-help groups are composed of individuals and a leader who focus on a particular topic. They may be designed for the enhancement of mental or physical health (e.g., weight control, smoking cessation, meditation), or they may be a form of ongoing therapy and provide a chance to help others with similar problems (e.g., Alcoholics Anonymous). Crisis or suicide prevention centers are staffed by professionals and trained paraprofessionals. Usually they are community funded and offer anonymity to callers. Generally, they are in operation 24 hours a day and may see walk-in clients.

A good source of information regarding any of these services can often be community mental health centers, which are generally listed in the local telephone directory. These are community agencies that provide mental health services and employ psychiatrists, psychologists, social workers, and other professionals. Most operate on a sliding scale, meaning that they charge at a rate that is commensurate with the person's financial resources. The many options available can be quite confusing to a lay person. Thus, referral information for specific agencies or practitioners can be very helpful.

Next, you will want to assist in developing a strategy for getting questions answered if the person does decide to seek assistance from a professional. An initial call can be made simply to clarify an individual provider's qualifications, expertise in the area in which the prospective client is experiencing difficulties, licensing, fees, and so on. Explain that good therapists will freely provide this information. An initial appointment generally consists of an interview or a discussion of the problem. During this first visit, one can expect a discussion of the types of treatment offered, a recommendation of psychological testing to further assist in evaluating one's difficulties, or possibly a referral to another professional. It is important to emphasize that a person who does not feel comfortable after the first contact, can, and should, investigate treatment with a different professional.

Many people are confused about the boundaries of confidentiality. Thus, you should explain that the things that are discussed with the mental health professional are generally held in confidence by law and cannot be disclosed without the client's permission. However, there are certain circumstances, particularly with employee assistance programs, use of inhouse therapists, and the like, where the individual should clarify whether problems discussed in therapy might be revealed to others (e.g., employers) and under what circumstances.

Other issues that people may wish to discuss with their therapist include the following.

1. *Fees.* Are the therapist's services covered by the individual's health insurance? Would the person be charged for an initial visit? Does the therapist charge for missed or cancelled sessions? What would the billing schedule be?

2. *Treatment Approach.* What types of treatment would be offered for the person's difficulties?

3. *Practical Concerns.* What hours would the therapist be available and would someone else be available in case of emergency if the therapist could not be reached? How long does the therapist expect treatment to last? How long would each session last? How often will they take place?

STRESS ANALYSIS FORM

Example (Jim)

1. Describe what <u>happened</u> in the situation.
   I got mad because all week I had been planning to work on my car and when I went to get my tools they were gone. Bob had borrowed them without asking me.

2. Describe what you were <u>feeling</u> during the situation.
   I felt angry and frustrated - like I was being prevented from doing what I had planned. I also noticed how tight my muscles felt, and about an hour later I had a horrible headache.

3. Describe your <u>self-statements</u> (thoughts) during the situation.
   I had thoughts like "Bob must be the most inconsiderate person I've ever known," and "Bob couldn't have done anything to make me more angry," and "I would never do something like that."

4. How did you want the situation to come out?
   At first, I just wanted to yell at him and get my tools back. Later I decided that I wanted to tell him how inconvenienced I had been, but without negatively affecting our friendship.

5. What were the positive and negative consequences of the outcome of the situation?

Negative	Positive
No work done on the car.	I didn't end up yelling at Bob.
I got upset, had a headache.	I learned how upset I get.
Snapped at my wife for something trivial.	I allowed myself to calm down before calling Bob.

6. In what ways would you have liked the situation to have turned out differently?
   I wish that I could have prevented myself from getting so upset that I was afraid to call Bob for fear of saying something horrible to him. I could have called him and just explained my situation to him and asked him to return my tools. I could have asked him to use the tools the next night instead. I also wish that I had not taken it out on my wife by snapping at her because she really didn't have anything to do with why I was upset.

59

STRESS ANALYSIS FORM

1. Describe what <u>happened</u> in the situation.

2. Describe what you were <u>feeling</u> during the situation.

3. Describe your <u>self-statements</u> (thoughts) during the situation.

4. How did you want the situation to come out?

5. What were the positive and negative consequences of the outcome of the situation?

        <u>Negative</u>   <u>Positive</u>

6. In what ways would you have liked the situation to have turned out differently?

CHAPTER 4.
WORKING WITH SPECIFIC
OCCUPATIONAL GROUPS

In recent years, corporations and businesses have directed efforts toward training their employees in techniques of stress management. Many larger agencies have either employed mental health professionals as in-house staff members or have designated certain personnel to be stress counselors/trainers. Other agencies have opted for utilizing outside consultants. In this chapter, we cover a few issues specific to working with homo-geneous occupational groups.

ROLE OF THE FACILITATOR

As a stress management facilitator for an occupa-tional group, you may recognize some of the stressful as-pects of specific occupations and are eager to get started in helping individuals manage their stress more effec-tively. However, despite your knowledge, familiarity with techniques, and dedication, you may not get through to people if you are not willing to examine your own limitations and to accept the fact that you *are not* an ex-pert! You may have worked in a similar profession for many years; you may be a renowned psychologist; you may have helped thousands to deal with stress - but you still have a lot to learn from each person with whom you work.

STEPS TO BEING EFFECTIVE
WITH OCCUPATIONAL GROUPS

Step One: Knowledge. The first step has to do with your familiarity and empathy with the position of the occupational group with which you are working. You must familiarize yourself with the general literature regarding stress and the specific occupational group. If you are working with law enforcement officers, for example, you will want to review the appropriate section in this chapter, Chapter 1 in *Stress Management Workbook for Law Enforcement Officers* (Belles & Norvell, 1990), and recent published work in such police journals as *The Police Chief*, *Journal of Police Science and Administration*, *Police Stress*, and *Criminal Justice and Behavior*. Goolkasian, Geddes, and DeJong (1986) offer a good review of the issues and practices in police stress and stress management. At the end of this chapter, we also provide a brief review of stress and the health-care professionals. Many health-related journals present relevant articles, including *Behavioral Medicine* (formerly the *Journal of Human Stress*), the *Journal of Occupational Medicine*, and *Research in Nursing and Health*.

After familiarizing yourself with the literature, turn to the more specific features of the population with whom you are working. For example, we have worked closely with the Florida Highway Patrol. In addition to the fact that their work resembles traditional police work in many ways, we also recognized that highway patrol officers face unique situations, including covering vast stretches of state highways, often with only distant backup; frequent interactions with hostile and ungrateful motorists; and a belief by other law enforcement officers that they do not perform "real" police work. Because each agency and profession differs to some degree, you will want to assess any unique needs for a stress management program. How do you learn about these? First, talk with the administrators in professions with which you will (or hope) to work. Ask them specific questions, such as:

• Of what kinds of stress do employees complain?
• What do you view as the most negative consequences of stress (e.g., absenteeism, alcohol/drug problems, poor morale, high turnover)?
• Why do you believe some workers deal more effectively with stress?

- What efforts have been made thus far to deal with stress (e.g., employee assistance programs, inhouse seminars, training of supervisors to deal with subordinates' stress, referral for counseling, physical fitness programs)?
- What has led to the current interest in possibly initiating a stress management program?

Second, learn from the employees. Spend time with them and hear what they view as their stress. Again, specific questions will provide you with a great deal of information.

- What do you find most stressful about the work you perform?
- Do you feel the administration is aware of the stress you are under?
- What do other fellow employees do to help themselves combat stress?
- What do you believe is the most helpful/harmful way of dealing with stress?
- Have you ever read about/attended stress management programs?
- Would you know if a colleague was going through a very stressful period or would he or she be able to hide it?
- What signs and symptoms of stress do employees generally show?
- What would you recommend to a colleague who is under stress?
- Ideally, what would you want from a stress management program?
- How would you feel about an "outside" consultant coming in to help you and the other employees manage stress?

Pay particular attention to the number and type of administrative and organizational concerns expressed. If the primary focus is the administration, a program geared toward helping the individual cope with stress may be regarded by the employees as something being "done" to them without attention being paid to the real problem. You may encounter an attitude of, "If the *real* problems were fixed, we wouldn't experience stress and wouldn't *need* stress management."

Finally, with permission from the agency, make time to follow an employee around on a typical day to get an idea of what the job involves. For example, with law enforcement officers, we suggest that you ride with an officer on at least one occasion. Riding in the patrol car will increase your familiarity with some typical aspects of police work. Even more important, you will learn about aspects of police work that are often forgotten - the mounds of paperwork, relations with other officers at the station, court appearances, administrative hassles, and so on.

Step Two: Assume the Role of Coach. Whether you are working with people in a 1-day seminar, in a week long course, or as an ongoing consultant, think of yourself as a coach. Step one emphasizes obtaining knowledge, but step two suggests that you humble yourself a bit and not assume or convey that you are an expert. Despite what has been written on stress and unique aspects of certain professions, nobody knows the stresses of their occupation as well as do the workers themselves. You are not an expert when it comes to their stress, and this should be the message you give from your very first interaction with participants. Just as the football coach studies the players, learns their strengths and weaknesses, and helps develop skills, you, too, are there to enhance skills. Does it make a difference whether you have experience in an occupation similar to that of the people whom you are helping? There is no hard evidence on which to answer this question, but there are advantages either way. For example, if you are not in the same profession, you may be unaware of the nuances of the profession, and participants may express such thoughts as, "You have no idea what my job is like, so how can you help me to cope with *my* stress?" However, if employed in the same field (particularly in the same place of employment), openness and candor may actually be inhibited. If you are in the same profession, you may also come across as already *knowing* what the problems are (and perhaps as unwilling to listen to their concerns).

Step Three: Know Your Limitations and Know When/How to Make Referrals. As mentioned before, our program can be utilized by a variety of professionals, including police supervisors, directors of employee assistance programs, counselors, and psychologists. However, as levels of training vary, before beginning your stress management program you must recognize your own limitations and how you can seek assistance. As a guideline, ask yourself the following questions.

1. Have I had formal training in stress management techniques? If the answer is No, we recommend that you familiarize yourself with professional and lay readings (see previous chapter), attend at least one professional seminar on stress management, and consult with a professional in the field.
2. Am I trained to recognize the difference between stress and more serious problems? It is very likely that you will encounter people facing very serious problems for whom stress management is simply not enough. If you are not a trained psychologist or psychiatrist, you may have difficulty in recognizing such individuals and knowing when to refer them for additional professional help. When you cover specific intervention techniques, you will also discuss professional help. However, throughout your work with participants, you should emphasize the option of additional psychological assistance.

SUGGESTED OUTLINE FOR A PROGRAM

There are several options for organizing the presentation of the program described here. Our recommendation is for an 8-week group (1½ hour sessions) or a 1-week intensive program (30 to 40 hours). The more time you have, the better, as you can then allow more time for role-playing and discussing stress analysis.

I. Introduction and Group Building

    A. Stress and your occupation
    B. Members' expectations regarding stress management and goals of this program
    C. Role of the leader/facilitator
    D. Relaxation exercise (we end each day with this)

II. Explaining the Concept of Stress

    A. Historical background
    B. Stress/illness model
    C. Signs and symptoms of stress in ourselves and others

III. Intervention Techniques

    A. Self-statements
    B. Stress analysis
    C. Communication skills

        1. Verbal and nonverbal elements
        2. Game playing
        3. Dealing with difficult people

    D. Changing Life-Style Behaviors

        1. Didactic presentation regarding health consequences of risk factors
        2. Basic behavioral principles
        3. Establishing a specific program

    E. Seeking Professional Help

IV. Program Evaluation

In the earlier part of this guide, we covered the explanation of stress and the intervention techniques. However, we would like to provide some additional information related to I. (Introduction and Group Building) and IV. (Program Evaluation).

INTRODUCTION AND GROUP BUILDING

The very first part of your stress program involves "hooking" the participants. As part of rapport building with the occupational stress group, we suggest that, following introductions, you ask each participant to tell the group how he or she became interested in the profession and chose to enter it. Thus, from the start, you are conveying that you are interested in *their* story. In turn, describe *your* professional background to participants, particularly your interest in stress. Investigate participants' perceptions of what stress management involves, and their expectations for the current program. Assess their goals for the program and describe for them which of their goals can reasonably be met via the program. This is the point at which many administrative/organizational stressors may be identified. Clearly point out that the program is designed to assist employees manage their personal reactions to stressors they might encounter in their work environment, and not to identify and rectify organizational concerns. While allowing some degree of "griping" among members of the group is important (and probably unavoidable), "finger pointing" and blaming should not be considered a primary goal of the program.

Furthermore, the program should not be considered a process group psychotherapy experience. Individual participants' experiences and reactions are an important part of the program; however, in-depth self-exploration is best pursued in other contexts. Explore the potential differences between this and other "inservice" training programs they have experienced. As compared with previous training, this program is likely to include considerably more personal involvement and input from participants. Inquire into how the participants were selected to join the group. Were they "told" to attend or did they volunteer? This is also the point at which you should establish yourself as credible (step one in being an effective facilitator) and seek to be accepted as their coach (step two). Thus, you will follow with didactic information relevant to stress in their specific occupation. At the conclusion of this chapter, we provide two sections dealing with specific occupations (law enforcement and health care). For other professions, you will need to acquaint yourself with the relevant literature.

PROGRAM EVALUATION

The program we have outlined in this manual consists of providing knowledge and teaching specific skills. We recommend a pre-/post-knowledge survey to help you assess how much your participants have learned (see "Information Survey," pp. 73-75). We also recommend that you administer a "Consumer Satisfaction Survey" (pp. 76-78) at the end of the program to provide feedback, which we have found useful in our work with law enforcement personnel. The information survey not only allows you to learn how much information is retained, but also affirms for the participants that there are things about stress of which they were unaware. If you are working with a group other than law enforcement, you will want to adapt the occupational questions so that they are relevant to the specific group with whom you are working. You will find that the Consumer Satisfaction Survey allows participants to evaluate the program in a nonthreatening format and will be applicable for most groups. This information can also be summarized and reported to supervisors and administration.

STRESS AND LAW ENFORCEMENT

In the previous section, we emphasized how important it is to be familiar with the literature regarding stress and the law enforcement profession if you should find yourself working with this occupational group. Indeed, as Chapter 1 in the *Stress Management Workbook for Law Enforcement Officers* (Belles & Norvell, 1990) points out, police work has often been described as one of the most stressful occupations. Our review of the literature describes many studies that have identified psychological and physical difficulties associated with this profession. We emphasize these findings in the *Workbook* because it is important to convey some scientific knowledge of stress and law enforcement, not just empathy with the law enforcement officer's position. However, as a facilitator, you may wish to be a bit more critical of what is known about stress and this occupation. Although there are many negative consequences of stress associated with the law enforcement profession, is this profession actually one of the most stressful? If you ask the typical officer, you will probably get a resounding Yes - a response that probably stems from personal experience as well as the popular hype about the stressful nature of police work. Interestingly, scientific investigations have yet to answer this question conclusively.

As described in this guide, the stressors often associated with police work include "inherent" stressors (e.g., threats to health and safety, changing levels of stimulation, hostile interactions with civilians); administrative and judicial stressors (e.g., poor equipment, excessive paperwork, court appearances); and societal stressors (lack of public support, close scrutiny of behavior, etc.). Physical illness has been linked to the stressful nature of the work, including cardiovascular diseases, cancer of the colon and liver, digestive dysfunction, hypertension, hemorrhoids, and headaches (Guralnick, 1963; Haynes, 1978; Jacobi, 1975; Milham, 1983; Trojanowicz, 1980; Violanti, Vena, & Marshall, 1986; Vulcano, Barnes, & Breen, 1983). Psychological problems, including depression, sleep difficulties, impaired sexual functioning, alcoholism, social withdrawal, suspiciousness and defensiveness, marital problems, and even suicide (Sewell, 1981), can have a profound effect on the individual and the family. Feelings of cynicism, inadequacy, and worthlessness may result from the frustrations experienced in the work, together with a perceived lack of support from society and peers. In summary, various reports have been published that describe the significant levels of stress experienced by law enforcement personnel and the deleterious effects of job-related stress.

In a critical review of police stress research, Malloy and Mays (1984) concluded that, despite the logical conclusion that police work is one of the most stressful occupations, the police stress hypothesis has very little sound empirical support. Although few would argue that police work is not stressful, the lack of well-controlled empirical studies leaves the question of whether police work is more or less stressful than other occupations unanswered. The soundest work done in this area does suggest that helplessness and feelings of uncontrollability in the work environment may be a major source of stress for police officers. Individual differences among law enforcement personnel certainly mediate the relationship between stress and illness. Such moderator factors include social support, genetic predisposing factors, and personality. Regardless of the comparative intensity of stress experienced by law enforcement personnel as a whole, the individual perception of stress warrants the continued development and implementation of stress management programs for this population.

Our discussion here does not mean that we disagree with the premise that law enforcement is a stressful occupation. We admire the persons who choose this profession and we recognize the need to help individuals cope with the stress that they experience. However, we also have come to believe that many occupations and situations in life involve significant stress that can be psychologically and physically harmful if not managed. Did we come to this realization through scientific investigation? Perhaps - but it is more likely that it came to us on the last day in one of our seminars when an officer marveled, "You know, I always thought that *I* was under so much stress because I'm a cop. But I'm beginning to realize that the old farmer out in his field probably experiences just as much stress when his tractor breaks down. I guess it's all in how you look at it and then deal with it."

STRESS AND THE
HEALTH-CARE PROFESSIONS

Increasing attention has been paid to the stress encountered by health-care professionals in the performance of their jobs. Job stress has been studied in many health professions, including nursing (Numerof & Adams, 1984), medicine (Roeske, 1981), and pharmacy (Wolfgang, 1988), and both the sources and the consequences of stress in these occupations have been identified. The potential impact of stress on job performance provides the major reason for the interest devoted to stress in the health-care professions. As Muldary (1983) describes, stress in these occupations can have an effect on the professional's commitment to providing care, as well as the individual's concentrational and problem-solving abilities, and can result in maladaptive coping patterns such as substance abuse. Burnout, which we described briefly earlier, has been almost exclusively associated with those in the helping professions, including health-care personnel (Perlman & Hartman, 1982).

Several stressful job characteristics unique to the health-care field have been identified, including the demands specific to patient care, handling medical crises, dealing with issues relating to death and dying, fitting into a health-care team or "hierarchy," and becoming emotionally attached to a favorite patient. The demands associated with a hectic work pace, role ambiguity, heavy patient loads, lack of challenge, and responsibility in the treatment of critically ill patients are additional stressors reported by health-care professionals. Chronic-care providers are often confronted with what they perceive to be treatment failures, which quickly undermine initial enthusiasm. The long-term consequences are typically thought to include attitudinal changes regarding one's place of employment and the patients one serves, including lessened sensitivity to patients' physical and emotional needs, as well as psychophysiological symptoms of somatic distress and illness, absenteeism, turnover, and grievances (Hammer et al., 1985).

Respiratory therapists are one group of health-care professionals with whom we have worked. Research has shown that these therapists often find that they are offered minimal input in planning patient care and they report feeling that their skills are not fully utilized

(Finch, 1982; Levine, 1982). In our work with respiratory therapists, we have found all of these factors operating in the perceived stress experienced in this occupation. However, participants also reported other sources of job dissatisfaction and stress that were not directly amenable to a program such as the one described in this guide, including a lack of assistance and cooperation from co-workers when needed, role ambiguities within the medical hierarchy, an inconsistent work schedule, and a lack of support and recognition from supervisors and other medical personnel. As we mentioned earlier, if the organizational environment is identified as the primary source of stress in an occupational group, a program such as this, which focuses on changing perceptions and developing coping mechanisms, not only may have a minimal impact, but also may be received unfavorably by participants. In those cases, stress management programs should be implemented only when done so in conjunction with organizational or job-change programs designed to modify such stressors.

In recent years, the identification and amelioration of occupational stress experienced by paramedics have gained the attention of mental health professionals. Identified sources of stress for paramedics include administrative issues, lack of supervisory support, role ambiguity, dealing with personal threats, the number of calls during a shift, relationships with the public, dangerous working conditions, and dealing with critically ill or injured people (Dutton et al., 1978; Elling, 1980; Graham, 1981; Mitchell, 1984; Page, 1980). In a more recent study, Allison et al. (1987) reported that paramedics identified lack of freedom on the job, poor recognition of their skills and efforts, work interference with family life, and feelings of being taken advantage of as contributing to their job stress. The consequences in terms of emotional, physiological, and behavioral changes appear to be similar to those of other stressful occupational groups. One study has reported that paramedics experience greater levels of perceived stress than other health-care personnel, and that the most frequent result is negative attitudes toward their patients and the organization for which they work, rather than psychophysiological signs of stress such as fatigue or sickness (Hammer et al., 1986). One interesting hypothesis is that the paramedic profession may attract people who are comfortable with more stressful environmental conditions.

One issue we have not yet addressed has to do with short-term crisis intervention versus stress management. Emergency medical and fire personnel are often involved in recovering, stabilizing, and evacuating victims of natural and other disasters. Police officers, in addition to responding to disasters, occasionally are personally involved in shootings. The emotional effects of these experiences and their implications for prevention and treatment are beyond the scope of this guide. Readers are referred to other sources for information in this area (e.g., Durham, McCammon, & Allison, 1985; Hoge & Hirschman, 1985; D. R. Jones, 1985; Markowitz et al., 1987; McFarlane, 1986).

INFORMATION SURVEY

1. According to research in the area of stress and law enforcement, which of the following factors associated with law enforcement is <u>least</u> often reported by police officers as contributing to the stress of their jobs?

    a. Constant shift changes
    b. Rapid shifts in activity level
    c. Feelings of always being on duty
    d. Fear of physical injury and death

2. List three physical illnesses or diseases that are more prevalent among law enforcement officers than in the general population.

    _____

    _____

    _____

3. List three psychological/emotional problems that are more prevalent among law enforcement officers than in the general population.

    _____

    _____

    _____

4. Which of the following statements is <u>true</u> of law enforcement officers relative to the general public?

    a. They have higher rates of hospitalization.
    b. They have higher rates of marital difficulties.
    c. They have higher rates of suicide.
    d. All of the above.

5. Which of the following statements is <u>true</u>?

    a. All law enforcement personnel will eventually experience the long-term negative health consequences of stress.
    b. The longer you are involved in law enforcement, the less likely you are to suffer from stress-related physical or psychological problems.
    c. Some people seem naturally to cope better with police stress and are less likely to suffer from a stress-related physical or psychological problem.
    d. Your ability to manage stress must be learned (in a special stress management course); it does not develop naturally.

6. True or False (circle one): Higher paying occupations are associated with lower levels of stress.

7. If you suspected that one of your fellow officers was significantly depressed, what are two signs or symptoms that you might expect to see that would indicate depression in that person?

   _____

   _____

8. What are five physical symptoms you might see in someone who is experiencing a great deal of stress (example - complaints of headaches)?

   _____

   _____

   _____

   _____

   _____

9. What are five mental or emotional changes that you might see in someone who is experiencing a great deal of stress (example - the person has begun to pay a lot less attention to details on his or her reports)?

   _____

   _____

   _____

   _____

   _____

10. What are five behaviors you might see in someone who is experiencing a great deal of stress (example - the person is calling in sick more often)?

   _____

   _____

   _____

   _____

   _____

11. What are three physical changes that you might experience in your body when you are confronted with a stressful situation?

_____

_____

_____

12. Name two things that a person may be doing that might contribute to high blood pressure.

_____

_____

13. Name five factors that have been identified as contributing to a decrease in the chances of developing cancer.

_____

_____

_____

_____

_____

14. What are two negative side effects of consuming caffeine?

_____

_____

15. In smokers who have stopped smoking before the onset of irreversible lung or heart disease, the body begins to repair itself. How many years of nonsmoking will it take before the risk of heart attack or lung cancer returns to that of a non-smoker?

   a. 1 year
   b. 5 years
   c. 10-15 years
   d. At least 20 years
   e. Never

16. If one of your colleagues came to you and told you that he or she was having problems handling stress, where or to whom would you recommend the person go for help?

_____

17. What would you do if you suspected that one of your fellow officers had an alcohol or drug abuse problem?

_____

CONSUMER SATISFACTION SURVEY

We would like your opinion concerning various aspects of the Stress Management Program you have just completed. This information is valuable in helping us determine the program's strengths and weaknesses and in what areas we might make changes.

1. Overall, the subject material of this program was:

    _____ very interesting
    _____ somewhat interesting
    _____ neither interesting nor uninteresting
    _____ somewhat uninteresting
    _____ very uninteresting

2. Overall, how helpful did you find the material presented in the program?

    _____ very helpful
    _____ somewhat helpful
    _____ neither helpful nor unhelpful
    _____ somewhat unhelpful
    _____ very unhelpful

3. Overall, how much information did you learn about stress management as a result of participating in this program?

    _____ a great deal
    _____ a lot
    _____ some
    _____ a little
    _____ none

4. The presentation of the material was:

    _____ excellent
    _____ good
    _____ adequate
    _____ marginal
    _____ poor

5. My knowledge of the concept of stress now is:

    _____ excellent
    _____ good
    _____ adequate
    _____ marginal
    _____ poor

6. My knowledge of identifying the symptoms of stress now is:

_____ excellent
_____ good
_____ adequate
_____ marginal
_____ poor

7. My overall knowledge of the specific techniques is:

_____ excellent
_____ good
_____ adequate
_____ marginal
_____ poor

8. My ability to use the specific intervention techniques is:

_____ excellent
_____ good
_____ adequate
_____ marginal
_____ poor

9. For each of the six intervention techniques presented, please indicate a rating of importance and relevance using the following scale.

1 = very important and useful technique for managing stress
2 = somewhat useful technique for managing stress
3 = perhaps a useful technique for managing stress
4 = probably not a very useful technique for managing stress
5 = definitely not a useful technique for managing stress

_____ Relaxation training
_____ Modifying self-statements
_____ Stress analysis
_____ Effective communication skills
_____ Changing life-style behaviors
_____ Seeking professional help

10. Of the six techniques listed previously, what could be substantially changed in presenting the technique to other personnel in your profession? (List the technique and change, i.e., more information, more examples, more reading, etc.)

11. Using the scale below, please rate each leader and/or co-leader.

    1 = excellent
    2 = good
    3 = adequate
    4 = marginal
    5 = poor

Leader_____   Co-Leader_____
                                    (If applicable)

      (fill in name)   (fill in name)

a. Knowledge of material _____
b. Ability to present
   material effectively _____   _____
c. interaction with
   group members   _____   _____

12. Would you recommend this class to other personnel in your profes-
    sion?

    _____ definitely
    _____ probably
    _____ maybe
    _____ probably not
    _____ definitely not

13. The major strength of the class was:

14. The major weakness of the class was:

REFERENCES

Allison, E. J., Whitley, T. W., Revicki, D. A., & Landis, S. S. (1987). Specific occupational satisfaction and stresses that differentiate paid and volunteer EMTs. *Annals of Emergency Medicine, 16,* 111-114.

Anchin, J. C., & Kiesler, D. J. (1982). *Handbook of Interpersonal Psychotherapy.* New York: Pergamon.

Appelson, G. (1983). Stress on stress: Compensator claims growing. *American Bar Association Journal, 69,* 142-152.

Ashley, F., & Kannel, W. (1974). Relation of weight change to changes in atherogenic traits: The Framingham Study. *Journal of Chronic Diseases, 27,* 103-114.

Belles, D., & Norvell, N. (1990). *Stress Management Workbook for Law Enforcement Officers.* Sarasota, FL: Professional Resource Exchange.

Benson, H. (1975). *The Relaxation Response.* New York: Avon.

Berne, E. (1967). *Games People Play.* New York: Grove Press.

Bernstein, D. A., & Borkovec, T. D. (1973). *Progressive Relaxation Training: A Manual for the Helping Professions.* Champaign, IL: Research Press.

Cautela, J. R., & Kastenbaum, R. (1967). A reinforcement survey schedule for use in therapy, training and research. *Psychological Reports, 20,* 1115-1130.

Centers for Disease Control. (1980). *Risk Factor Update.* Atlanta: U.S. Department of Health and Human Services.

Cobb, S., & Rose, R. M. (1973). Hypertension, peptic ulcer, and diabetes in air traffic controllers. *Journal of the American Medical Association, 224,* 489-492.

Cooper, C. L. (1983). Identifying stressors at work: Recent research developments. *Journal of Psychosomatic Research, 27,* 369-376.

Cooper, C. L., Davidson, M. J., & Robinson, P. (1982). Stress in the police service. *Journal of Occupational Medicine, 24,* 30-36.

Durham, T. W., McCammon, S. L., & Allison, E. J. (1985). The psychological impact of disaster on rescue personnel. *Annals of Emergency Medicine, 14,* 73-77.

Dutton, L. M., Smolensky, M. H., Lorimer, R., et al. (1978). Psychological stress levels in paramedics. *Emergency Medical Services, 7,* 88-94.

Elling, R. (1980). Stress as related to the EMT-P. *EMT Journal, 4,* 32-34.

Fell, R. D., Richard, W. D., & Wallace, W. L. (1980). Psychological job stress and the police officer. *Journal of Police Science and Administration, 8,* 139-144.

Fielding, J. E. (1982). Effectiveness of employee health improvement programs. *Journal of Occupational Medicine, 24,* 907-916.

Finch, J. S. (1982). Who's in control here? An editorial. *Respiratory Therapy, 13,* 13.

French, J. R. (1975). A comparative look at stress and strain in policemen. In W. H. Kroes & J. J. Hurrell, Jr. (Eds.), *Job Stress and the Police Officer: Identifying Stress Reduction Techniques* (pp. 76-187). Washington, DC: HEW Publication No. (NIOSH).

Girdano, D. (1986). *Occupational Health Promotion.* New York: Macmillan.

Goethals, G. R., & Worchel, S. (1981). *Adjustment and Human Relationships.* New York: Alfred A. Knopf.

Goolkasian, G. A., Geddes, R. W., & DeJong, W. (1986). *Coping with Police Stress.* Washington, DC: U.S. Government Printing Office.

Graham, N. K. (1981). Done in, fed up, burned out: Too much attention in EMS. *Journal of Emergency Medical Services, 6,* 24-29.

Greenberg, J. S. (1983). *Comprehensive Stress Management.* Dubuque, IA: William C. Brown Company.

Guralnick, L. (1963). Mortality by occupation and cause of death among men 20-64 years of age, 1950. *United States Public Health Service Vital Statistics Special*

Report, 53. Washington, DC: U.S. Government Printing Office.

Hammer, J. S., Jones, J. W., Lyons, J. S., Sixsmith, D., & Afficiando, E. (1985). Measurement of occupational stress in hospital settings: Two validity studies of a measure of self-reported stress in medical emergency rooms. *General Hospital Psychiatry, 7,* 156-162.

Hammer, J. S., Mathews, J. J., Lyons, J. S., & Johnson, N. J. (1986). Occupational stress within the paramedic profession: An initial report of stress levels compared to hospital employees. *Annals of Emergency Medicine, 15,* 45-48.

Haynes, W. D. (1978). *Stress Related Disorders in Policemen.* San Francisco: R & E Research Associates.

Hoge, M. A., & Hirschman, R. (1985). Psychological skills for emergency medical technicians: A training guide. In P. A. Keller & L. G. Ritt (Eds.), *Innovations in Clinical Practice: A Source Book* (Vol. 4, pp. 377-390). Sarasota, FL: Professional Resource Exchange.

Holmes, T. H., & Rahe, R. H. (1967). The social readjustment rating scale. *Journal of Psychosomatic Research, 11,* 213-218.

Jacobi, J. (1975). Reducing police stress: A psychiatrist's point of view. In W. H. Kroes & J. J. Hurrell, Jr. (Eds.), *Job Stress and the Police Officer: Identifying Stress Reduction Techniques* (pp. 76-187). Washington, DC: HEW Publication No. (NIOSH).

Jacobson, E. (1938). *Progressive Relaxation.* Chicago: University of Chicago Press.

Jones, D. R. (1985). Secondary disaster victims: The emotional effects of recovering and identifying human remains. *American Journal of Psychiatry, 142,* 303-307.

Kiesler, D. J. (1986). Interpersonal methods of diagnosis and treatment. In J. O. Cavenar (Ed.), *Psychiatry* (pp. 1-23). Philadelphia: Lippincott.

Knapp, M. L. (1978). *Nonverbal Communication in Human Interaction.* New York: Holt, Rinehart & Winston.

Kroes, W. H. (1976). *Society's Victim--The Policeman: An Analysis of Job Stress in Policing.* Springfield, IL: Charles C. Thomas.

Kroes, W. H., & Hurrell, J. J., Jr. (Eds.). (1975). *Job Stress and the Police Officer: Identifying Stress Reduction Techniques.* Washington, DC: HEW Publication No. (NIOSH).

Kroes, W. H., Hurrell, J. J., Jr., & Margolis, B. (1974). Job stress in police administration. *Journal of Police Science and Administration, 2,* 145-155.

Lamburth, L. (1984). An employee assistance program that works. *The Police Chief, 51,* 36-38.

LaRiviere, L., & Sanchez, C. (1984). A day in the lives of respiratory therapists in the NICU. *Respiratory Therapy, 14,* 59-62.

Lawrence, R. (1984). Police stress and personality factors: A conceptual model. *Journal of Criminal Justice, 12,* 247-263.

Levine, E. R. (1982). Responsibility should equal training. *Respiratory Therapy, 14,* 14.

Levine, E. R. (1986). A gap in patient care. Respiratory Therapy, 16, 11.

Malloy, T. E., & Mays, G. L. (1984). The police stress hypothesis: A critical evaluation. *Criminal Justice and Behavior, 11,* 197-224.

Markowitz, J. S., Gutterman, E. M., Link, B., & Rivera, M. (1987). Psychological response of firefighters to a chemical fire. *Journal of Human Stress,* Summer, 84-93.

Maslach, C. (1982). *Burnout: The Cost of Caring.* Englewood Cliffs, NJ: Prentice-Hall.

Maslach, C., & Jackson, S. E. (1981). *Maslach Burnout Inventory Manual.* Palo Alto, CA: Consulting Psychologists Press.

Maslach, C., & Pines, A. (1977). The burnout syndrome in the day care setting. *Child Care Quarterly, 6,* 100-113.

Mattingly, M. A. (1977). Sources of stress and burnout in professional care work. *Child Care Quarterly, 6,* 127-137.

McCullough, J. P. (1980). How to help depressed patients gain control over their lives using a situational analysis procedure. *Behavioral Medicine, 7,* 33-34.

McFarlane, A. C. (1986). Long-term psychiatric morbidity after a natural disaster. *The Medical Journal of Australia, 145,* 561-563.

Milham, S. (1983). *Occupational Mentality in Washington State, 1950-59* (DHHS [NIOSH] Publication No. 83-116). Washington, DC: U.S. Government Printing Office.

Mitchell, J. T. (1984). The 600-run limit. *Journal of Emergency Medical Services, 9,* 52-54.

Muldary, T. W. (1983). *Burnout and Health Professionals: Manifestations and Management.* Norwalk, CT: Appleton-Century-Crofts.

Murphy, L. R. (1984). Occupational stress management: A review and appraisal. *Journal of Occupational Psychology, 57,* 1-15.

Norvell, N., & Belles, D. R. (1987). A stress management curriculum for law enforcement personnel supervisors. *The Police Chief, 54,* 57-59.

Numerof, R. E., & Adams, M. N. (1984). Sources of stress among nurses: An empirical investigation. *Journal of Human Stress, 10,* 88-100.

Page, J. O. (1980). Burnout: The most probable causes and the most likely solutions. *EMT Journal, 4,* 52-54.

Perlman, B., & Hartman, E. A. (1982). Burnout: Summary and future research. *Human Relations, 35,* 283-305.

Pollack, M. L., & Gettman, L. L. (1976). *Coronary Risk Factors and Level of Physical Fitness in Police Officers.* Proceedings of the 83rd Annual Conference of the International Association of Chiefs of Police, Miami, FL.

Pullen, E. (1981). Coping with burnout in respiratory therapists. *Respiratory Therapy, 11,* 93-96.

Reinertsen, J. (1983). Promoting health is good business. *Occupational Health and Safety, 52,* 18-22.

Reiser, M. (1974). Stress, distress, and adaptation in police work. *The Police Chief, 43,* 24-27.

Reiser, M. (1976). Some organizational stresses on policemen. *Journal of Police Science and Administration, 2,* 156-159.

Richard, W. C., & Fell, R. D. (1975). Health factors in police stress. In W. H. Kroes & J. J. Hurrell, Jr. (Eds.), *Job Stress and the Police Officer: Identifying Stress Reduction Techniques* (pp. 76-187). Washington, DC: HEW Publication No. (NIOSH).

Roeske, N. C. A. (1981). Stress and the physician. *Psychiatric Annals, 11,* 245-249.

Russek, H. J., & Russek, L. G. (1976). Is emotional stress an etiological factor in coronary heart disease? *Psychosomatics, 17,* 63.

Sarason, I. G., Johnson, J. H., & Siegel, J. M. (1978). Assessing the impact of life changes. Development of the life experiences survey. *Journal of Consulting and Clinical Psychology, 46,* 932-946.

Selye, H. (1936). *The Stress of Life.* New York: McGraw-Hill.

Selye, H. (1974). *Stress Without Distress.* New York: J. B. Lippincott.

Sewell, J. D. (1981). Police stress. *FBI Law Enforcement Bulletin, 50,* 7-11.

Sharit, J., & Salvendy, G. (1982). Occupational stress: Review and appraisal. *Human Factors, 24,* 129-162.

Taber, M. (1984). Job burnout rates higher for social service professions. *Occupational Health and Safety, 51,* 52.

Territo, L., & Vetter, H. J. (Eds.). (1981). *Stress and Police Personnel.* Boston, MA: Allyn and Bacon.

Trojanowicz, R. C. (1980). *The Environment of the First-Line Police Supervisor.* Englewood Cliffs, NJ: Prentice-Hall.

Violanti, J. M. (1983). Stress patterns in police work: A longitudinal study. *Journal of Police Science and Administration, 11,* 211-216.

Violanti, J. M., & Marshall, J. R. (1983). The police stress process. *Journal of Police Science and Administration, 11,* 389-394.

Violanti, J. M., Vena, J. E., & Marshall, J. R. (1986). Disease risk and mortality among police officers: New evidence and contributing factors. *Journal of Police Science and Administration, 14,* 17-23.

Vulcano, B. A., Barnes, G. E., & Breen, L. J. (1983). The prevalence and predictors of psychosomatic symptoms and conditions among police officers. *Psychosomatic Medicine, 45,* 277-293.

Watzlawick, P., Beavin, J. H., & Jackson, D. D. (1960). *Pragmatics of Human Communication.* New York: Norton.

Weiman, C. G. (1977). A study of occupational stressors and the incidence of disease/risk. *Journal of Occupational Medicine, 19,* 119-122.

White, J. W., Lawrence, P. S., Biggerstaff, C., & Grubb, T. D. (1985). Factors of stress among police officers. *Criminal Justice and Behavior, 12,* 111-128.

Wolfgang, A. P. (1988). Job stress in the health professions: A study of physicians, nurses and pharmacists. *Behavioral Medicine,* Spring, 43-47.

Woolfolk, R. L., & Lehrer, P. M. (Eds.). (1984). *Principles and Practice of Stress Management.* New York: Guilford.

ADDITIONAL LAY AND PROFESSIONAL READINGS

Bolton, R. (1979). *People Skills: How to Assert Yourself, Listen to Others and Resolve Conflicts.* New York: Simon & Schuster.

Charlesworth, E., & Nathan, R. G. (1982). *Stress Management: A Comprehensive Guide to Wellness.* New York: Ballantine.

Ciminero, A. R. (1986). *One Minute Stress Management.* Miami: Ciminero & Associates.

Cooper, C. L. (1981). *The Stress Check.* Englewood Cliffs, NJ: Prentice-Hall.

Cooper, K. H. (1977). *The Aerobics Way.* Philadelphia: M. Evans/Lippincott.

Elgin, S. H. (1980). *The Gentle Art of Verbal Self-Defense.* Dorset Press.

Ellis, A., & Harper, R. (1975). *A New Guide to Rational Living.* Los Angeles: Wilshire.

Emery, G., & Campbell, J. (1986). *Rapid Relief from Emotional Distress.* New York: Rawson Associates.

Friedman, M., & Rosenman, R. (1974). *Type A Behavior and Your Heart.* New York: Alfred A. Knopf.

Gmelch, W. H. (1982). *Beyond Stress to Effective Management.* New York: Wiley.

Jacobson, E. (1978). *You Must Relax.* New York: McGraw-Hill.

Keating, C. J. (1984). *Dealing with Difficult People.* New York: Paulist Press.

Lange, A., & Jakubowski, P. (1980). *Responsible Assertive Behavior.* Champaign, IL: Research Press.

85

Maslach, C. (1982). *Burnout: The Cost of Caring.* Englewood Cliffs, NJ: Prentice-Hall.

McCullough, J. P. (1984). Cognitive-behavioral analysis system of psychotherapy: An interactional treatment approach for dysthymic disorder. *Psychiatry, 47,* 234-250.

McLean, A. A. (1986). *High Tech Survival Kit: Managing Your Stress.* New York: Wiley.

Meichenbaum, D. (1985). *Stress Inoculation Training.* New York: Pergamon.

Rathus, S. A., & Nevid, J. S. (1977). *Behavior Therapy Strategies for Solving Problems in Living.* New York: Signet.

Roskies, E. (1987). *Stress Management for the Healthy Type A.* New York: Guilford.

Selye, H. (1974). *Stress Without Distress.* New York: J. B. Lippincott.